Caring, Empathy, and the Commons

People are not autonomous individuals but connected beings. *Curae ergo sum* – we care, therefore we are. Relationality – which refers to the ethic and manner by which relational considerations govern decisions and institutional arrangements can take advantage of the power of connection – uncovers how social connection, across divides, moves people to act for the other. Drawing from research on empathy, social networks, and determinants of pro-social behavior, *Caring, Empathy, and the Commons* builds on Ostrom's *Governing the Commons*. It offers a different mechanism by which collective action is induced, arguing that, sometimes, the individual thinks not in terms of individual gain but in terms of the other. Developing this concept of relationality, this book explores various strands of literature and examines how this idea might be used to foster collective action around climate, species protection, fair trade, and other dilemmas of the commons.

Raul P. Lejano is Professor of environmental education at New York University. His research revolves around two sides of relationality: how connectedness fosters collective action and disconnectedness increases vulnerability. He is a coauthor, with Wing Shan Kan, of a book entitled *Relationality: The Inner Life of Public Policy* (Cambridge University Press).

Caring, Empathy, and the Commons

A Relational Theory of Collective Action

RAUL P. LEJANO
New York University

CAMBRIDGE
UNIVERSITY PRESS

Shaftesbury Road, Cambridge CB2 8EA, United Kingdom

One Liberty Plaza, 20th Floor, New York, NY 10006, USA

477 Williamstown Road, Port Melbourne, VIC 3207, Australia

314–321, 3rd Floor, Plot 3, Splendor Forum, Jasola District Centre,
New Delhi – 110025, India

103 Penang Road, #05–06/07, Visioncrest Commercial, Singapore 238467

Cambridge University Press is part of Cambridge University Press & Assessment,
a department of the University of Cambridge.

We share the University's mission to contribute to society through the pursuit of
education, learning and research at the highest international levels of excellence.

www.cambridge.org
Information on this title: www.cambridge.org/9781316518779

DOI: 10.1017/9781009003353

First published 2023

A catalogue record for this publication is available from the British Library.

*A Cataloging-in-Publication data record for this book is available from the
Library of Congress*

ISBN 978-1-316-51877-9 Hardback

Contents

Figures

Tables

Preface and Acknowledgments

It felt like the right time to write this book. It is, in part, a reflection of a series of related, but distinct, lines of research – on collective action, policy analysis, social/environmental justice, and climate action. While they were all closely related, each was done separately from the other, and it seemed time to connect these ideas and bring them into one coherent work.

I have worked two sides of a coin – studying connectedness on one side and disconnectedness on the other. One side of the argument is the idea that from connection can emerge collective action. The other side of it is a logically diametric idea, which disconnection alienates. My longstanding grounding in environmental justice work has taught me, if nothing else, just how much injustice stems from the radical separation of self from the other. But it was only not long ago that I came to realize just how much the two lines of research, on collective action and environmental injustice, were part of (in my case) the same work. Why did it take all those years to realize that the two would inevitably come together? I am not sure why. Some things take time.

Many of the central ideas of the book came from much earlier work, including my first book, *Frameworks for Policy Analysis: Merging Text and Context*, and an article on (curiously) turtles and institutions, entitled "The phenomenon of collective action: Modeling institutions as structures of care." The theoretical treatment of collective action reflects my earliest studies with Lloyd Shapley on mostly cooperative games. These early ideas evolved with a series of collaborations with like-minded colleagues. There was an article on bisons and other-regard with Helen Ingram and a subsequent book, *The Power of Narrative in Environmental Networks*, with Helen and Mrill Ingram. There was a defining article on climate and everyday knowledge with Fikret Berkes and Joana Tavares, drawing insight from Fikret's work on traditional ecological knowledge. I benefit greatly from my ongoing collaboration with Dan Stokols on social ecology and environmental justice, including a case study of a landfill in California. There were also important collaborations with Erualdo Gonzalez on social differencing and with Francisco Fernandez on the invisible hand of community. Central, too, was a book on climate action/inaction, entitled *The Power of Narrative: Climate Skepticism and the Deconstruction of Science*, co-authored with Shondel Nero, building on earlier collaboration with Jennifer Dodge. Most recent was a book with Wing Shan Kan entitled *Relationality: The Inner Life of Public Policy*.

I am grateful to Robert Dreesen for seeing the idea in this book and shepherding it through Cambridge University Press. I thank an anonymous reviewer who painstakingly pored through the first draft and helped me refine the writing considerably, as well as another who reviewed the book proposal. Thanks, too, to Erika Walsh for managing the review process and to Thirumangai Thamizhmani and Jessica Norman for the production.

I am forever grateful for the love and encouragement I receive from my mother, Alice Lejano, who taught psychology, my wife Wing Shan Kan, who teaches social work, and Baobao, who is her own excuse for being.

This book was written during a time of profound disconnect, when the world retreated into individual caves of isolation and is only now emerging into reencounter. While the pandemic is, hopefully, waning, social and ideological divisions run deeper than ever. Connection and reconnection – these are not novel concepts, but as a policy scholar, I see the need for new ideas for establishing and deepening connectedness in a world where, as Yeats wrote, things fall apart and the center does not hold. As my mother taught me, I think it is not unreasonable to live in a time of nihilism and, yet, to live in a spirit of hope.

I

Introduction

Caring for the Commons

In a classroom in Wallenpaupack, Pennsylvania, a teacher has his fifth-grade class link up online with another classroom in Kibera, Nairobi, halfway around the world. Looking at each other through the screen, the two groups think of something to do. They talk. His class sings a song that they had been practicing for St. Patrick's Day. The students in Nairobi sing back to them their national anthem in Swahili. Just another ordinary day in class, except for the oceans between them. The call ends, and both classes retreat to their respective continents. The teacher in Pennsylvania turns to his students, and he sees tears in their eyes.

What is it about the otherwise ordinary meeting that so moved those children (and their teacher)? It was just another day in class, after all. What is it about these commonplace moments of everyday life that move us?

This book is about the wonder of connection. A child looks at the monitor and sees, beyond the screen, another child on the other side looking at her, and in that moment, there is the experience of connectedness. There is another person there; I look at her, and she looks at me, and it's no longer simply a gaze but an encounter.

What happens in that moment? As we will explore in the book, in that brief encounter, we no longer just have two individuals in the world, floating like random atoms in space, but two beings somehow bound. Having so encountered the other, I am no longer simply myself, sitting with my solitary thoughts and concerns. Rather, I find myself feeling, thinking, and wondering about, and with, the *other*. Early phenomenologists called it intentionality. Speaking of atoms, it's like a single hydrogen atom floating by itself in space – a condition unstable enough that chemists refer to it as a free radical. When two such free radicals bump into each other, they invariably form a covalent bond and, at that point, float around in space as the hydrogen molecule that we know and cherish. All chemistry aside, what we have in an encounter is the emergence of relationship.

Connectedness

The main idea behind the book is that a powerful mechanism exists, which can foster collective action, one that has not received systematic treatment in the commons (and political economy) literature. Connection, whether face to face or virtual, whether formal or informal, can build empathy. Empathy, in turn, encourages people to think, feel, and act relationally – that is, to care for the welfare of one's self as well as the other. This mode of being and thinking, which we term relationality, is a natural condition. Furthermore, there are ways to foster this kind of relationality in all sorts of institutional contexts. Some circumstances foster relational thinking and being, while other situations, or institutions, suppress it. We cannot expect busy people in the busy city to act on the problem of melting glaciers a world away – unless they care. In this book, we develop a formal model of relationality and proceed to study the evidence supporting it and the ways we already see it at work in real-world situations. Toward the end of the book, we explore the idea that relationality often does not act in lieu of other strategies (such as market-centered or state-centered or community-centered approaches to fostering collective action) but complements them in vital ways.

This knowledge of, and connection with, an other can evolve into care. The other being now matters. Care is a powerful thing. It affects who I am and what I do in life. The many thinkers and writers who have drawn our attention to the phenomenon of care provide an antidote to the conventional presumption, which we have built into our cultural and institutional fabric, that people primarily go about their business looking out for themselves. But, as philosophers and psychologists alike have argued, care is a natural human condition. Our tendency, upon encountering another, is to care. When we develop an empathy for the other, we can hardly avoid beginning to act on it. This book is about the human potential for care and the promise it holds in the face of the many challenges confronting the world today.

It starts with making a connection. When we speak of an "other," we don't mean an abstract being but an individual, flesh-and-blood human (or nonhuman) being. Charitable organizations have practiced this theory without ever conceptualizing it, as they have learned from experience that people respond to charitable appeals when they learn not about some general condition but about the specific people in need. In many cases, they connect potential donors directly with individuals in need.[1] One might frame this as marketing strategy, but a more accurate description is that it is a recognition of each person's need for connection. Once we connect, not to an idea or a general situation, but to the specific other, then we begin to exhibit what has been referred to as other-regard.

Coffee Means People and Nature

HOPE Coffee is a coffee retailer that practices Direct Trade, which strives to link the coffee buyer directly to the farmer. Logistically, they deal with the farmers directly, usually financing some of the farmer's expenses up front and removing the need for middlemen. In human terms, they try to connect buyer and farmer in different ways. On their website*, one can read about Norma and Armando, fourth generation farmers in Guatemala, who used their funds to start a school for farmers' children, and listen to Rodimiro of Honduras, who hopes to share his knowledge of coffee with growers from other countries. One can buy a box of coffee and see a picture of the farmer who grew the beans in it. Buyers can even send messages of encouragement to the farmers.

As Kaysi Stanley (marketing manager for HOPE Coffee) explains, it's done this way because it's not just a financial transaction. "A good way to describe it is we have a relationship with our farmers ... I've been to Honduras, I have met Rodimiro ... that relationship is really key because ... we know about the farmer and their family and their struggles and what they want to happen ... [And] they know us ... that we're not going to move away from them and our relationship with them."

Why would they show a picture of the farmer on a box of coffee? She explains:

When you buy a bag [of coffee] at the grocery store. Nobody really thinks about where it came from ... [but] To pick up a bag of coffee and see the

---

[1] Some charities (e.g., World Vision) individually match donors and recipients.

picture and the name of the farmer who grew the coffee and see the link where I can go to and read the stories about where and what my dollars went to ... where it goes because now the family has a home, now this child has an education ... that's a completely different thing ... So when you buy a bag of coffee, you see the farmer.

The group also uses its proceeds to support civic projects in the farm communities. The organization is the natural point of contact between supplier and buyer, but they want the customer to have an even more direct link to the grower.

How do we make our customers feel more connected to the farmers, to where the coffee is coming from? And how do we make them feel a part of it, because they absolutely are ... We wouldn't be able to do these things like build homes and distribute water filters and put remove some school buildings. We wouldn't be able to do that without the customers.

Later in this book, we take up the example of Direct and Fair Trade coffee as an illustration of some of the ways relationality is already being employed in everyday settings.

* www.hopecoffee.com/meet-the-farmers/, accessed June 1, 2022.

The idea of caring for and about the other is closely related to the idea of collective action. Many problems in the world (poverty, crime, environmental squalor) are framed as issues that could be solved if only we could cooperate with one another and act for the greater good. The greater good, moreover, consists of those things that help not just you or me but all of us. For example, the City of New York expends much time and effort to pick up 1.7 million tons of litter from its streets and sidewalks each week; during the summer, the parks department removes 120 tons of litter each day from beaches and open spaces.[2] The logic of the collective action problem is straightforward: For each individual, it takes the least effort to just drop litter by the wayside instead of having to look for a receptacle. True, there are costs to littering, but these are mostly borne by other people, not just the litterer. And no one bothers to pick up the litter because they are waiting for someone else to do it (the free rider problem). The same logic can be applied to any number of situations. The world would have so much more of its tropical rainforests intact were it not for illegal loggers who flaunt the norms and remove

[2] www1.nyc.gov/html/dep/html/press_releases/17-054pr.shtml

many hectares of forest each year (Gutierrez-Velez & MacDicken, 2008). Again, the benefits are received by the individual loggers, while everyone else (including future generations) bear most of the costs. The coronavirus pandemic was undoubtedly worsened due to young adults eschewing face masks, because the greatest beneficiaries of such preventive action were not themselves but the people around them, particularly the most vulnerable (Vale et al., 2020). Olson's collective action concept (Olson, 1965) and Hardin's environmental representation of this, the tragedy of the commons (Hardin, 1968), have proven great pedagogic tools for understanding a multitude of issues.

How do we solve such collective action problems? Enter Elinor Ostrom. In her pioneering book, *Governing the Commons*, Ostrom wrote about classic solutions to collective action, which revolve around the market and the state, and she added a third: community (Ostrom, 1990). She began her treatise with the conventional wisdom that, to induce individuals to act for the collective good, the state would need to regulate their behavior or, alternatively, a market be created such that the individuals are charged the monetary value of the disbenefit created by their behavior.[3] However, as Ostrom reasoned, these games are not simply played once but repeatedly, and in repeated play, others can exert social (or other) sanctions on individuals until they learn to act responsibly. In other words, as long as there exists some form of community that can set rules for acceptable behavior, monitor individual behavior, and sanction rule violations, then cooperation can be maintained without the state or the market. She and colleagues then proceeded to illustrate communitarian action with an impressive set of case studies (e.g., Benjamin et al., 1994; Agrawal & Ostrom, 2001; Dietz, Ostrom, & Stern, 2002; Poteete, Janssen, & Ostrom, 2010; Gutiérrez, Hilborn, & Defeo, 2011; Andersson, Chang, & Molina-Garzón, 2020, to name a few).

While upholding the veracity of Ostrom's collective action model, this book looks at yet other routes by which cooperation emerges. For one thing, we find many situations (as we will present) where there is no semblance of a community that can set rules and levy sanctions – and yet, individuals often act for the greater good. Some of the common literature describes cases where sanctions were not predominant, yet long-standing collective action was maintained (e.g., De Moor & Tukker, 2015). Later in her career, Ostrom's work began to be more appreciative of other

---

[3] Conversely, the individual can be paid to reduce such behavior, in the amount equal to the offset damages (Baumol & Oates, 1988).

mechanisms that motivated individuals to act for the collective good. For example, Poteete, Janssen, and Ostrom (2010) describe case studies where individuals are driven not by external pressure imposed upon them but by norms that the individuals themselves had internalized. Presumably, these norms still require some form of community to generate such norms over time. In this literature, norms work like another form of rule system like Ostrom described. However, there are other situations, which we will take up, when other-regarding behavior emerges apart from any discernible transmission or adoption of rules and rule-like norms and apart from any coherent semblance of a community.

In this book, we explore this other phenomenon, which is how a person, realizing a connection with the other, begins to care for the other's welfare and, so, adjusts her behavior accordingly. To be as specific as possible, by connection, we don't simply evoke a feeling of belonging to a group or a sense of responsibility for a common good – what we mean is a person's direct connection with another.[4] Out of that connection arises a degree of empathy, which is an awareness of what the other experiences, feels, and thinks. Then, from empathy arises what we will refer to as other-regarding behavior. It is the transformation of individual cognition from one where she is cognizant of her own individual needs and wants to one where her decisions take into account not only her own needs and wants but the others' as well. It is driven by connectedness, which can arise from membership in a community. Connection can also arise even when no coherent community exists; in these cases, we can use the more general language of the social network, which is simply some group of interconnected individuals. Networks need not be rule-setting and sanctioning communities.

The potential of mere connection has not been looked into deeply enough. For example, the conventional wisdom is that face-to-face contact improves cooperation because individuals are able to coordinate their strategies (e.g. Falk, Fehr, & Fischbacher, 2002; Anderies et al., 2011). While the conventional wisdom is undoubtedly true, less appreciated is the effect of personal contact on the person's cognition of the other's perspective – in other words, its effect on empathy. It is undoubtedly true that collaborative, co-determinative modes of policymaking work because they allow trust and reputational effects that assure participants that people will abide by agreed-upon rules, but they also often work

---

[4] Our treatment of relationality remains open to the whole continuum between Benhabib's notions of the generalized versus concrete other (Benhabib, 1992), where the generalized other pertains to a being with rights and moral status, while the concrete other pertains to the unique individual with unique life histories, dispositions, needs, and wants.

because participants learn to put themselves in the shoes of the other, which is one route to empathy.

In Ostrom and colleagues' case studies, community most often revolved around propinquity, kinship, shared history, homophily, or other determinants of a categorical group. However, in many instances of cooperative behavior in the world of today, we often find no strong semblance of such a community that might set rules and coerce individuals to follow them.

Millions of collective action problems are solved each day, mostly without the intervention of government, market, or community. In these instances, individuals act not because of some external reward or sanction but in response to something internal (or, as we will expound on, something relational). As will be taken up in subsequent chapters, researchers make fine distinctions between different kind of internal motivations. There is the so-called warm glow of giving, a hedonic pleasure a person feels from being charitable. Yet, another internal motivation is a person's moral compass. In addition to these, there is a kind of internal motivation that emerges from the personal encounter one has with the other, and it is the condition of empathy. We will be more precise about what we mean by these terms in later chapters, but empathy can be understood as some awareness or concern for what the other experiences. In some other literature on collective action, this can also be referred to as other-regard. Empathy, in turn, can lead to relationality, which describes how one's behavior is mindful of the other.[5]

In this book, we formulate a relational model of decision-making. Relationality, which we will define in decision-theoretic terms in Chapter 2, pertains to the condition where a decision-maker makes choices based not only on her own individual welfare (or utility) but also on the others'. A more general definition of relationality is the condition whereby a person's thoughts, actions, and very being are influenced by one's relationship with the other. We will use the term, the *other*, to mean any person (or animal or thing) other than one's

[5] Note that altruism, which means acting solely for the good of the other or even sacrificing one's own benefit for the benefit of the other, is just one of many different conditions that are subsumed under the idea of relationality. Relationality simply posits that one's thoughts, actions, and being are influenced by the relationship with the other. Relationships are complex, as we will discuss later, and can be a complex of motives (including egoistic ones).

self. In institutional terms, relationality pertains to how a system (e.g., a commons) is governed with relational actors. The main requirement, for decision-makers to assume a relational perspective, is empathy, which is the person's ability or inclination to care for the welfare of the other. Secondly, we underscore how connectedness, which is the establishing of some linkage from one person to the other, engenders empathy (and, as a result, cooperation).

The beauty of connectedness is that, in many cases, it does not take much for a person to feel a connection. A sense of connection (or identification) can emerge from almost any kind of interaction. Getting to know someone in person is a natural opportunity to establish a connection, but linking people can occur over distances through digital media as well. Sometimes, all it takes, to trigger other-regard, is some kind of indirect contact with the other, such as reading about a person, seeing a photograph or video, or even knowing the person's name. It is the realization that there is another person there, which is not far behind the thought that this person, like me, has thoughts and feelings and hopes and fears just as I do. The person moves from objectifying the other, as a category or thing, to humanizing – that is, appreciating the presence of a kindred mind (Fiske, 2009). There is, as will be reviewed later in this book, considerable evidence from the psychology and neuroscience literature of how people naturally empathize (to the point of feeling what the other person feels) when just shown a picture of a person in some situation of pain or other condition.

The human ability to relate seems boundless.[6] Works of fiction have shown great potential for building empathy for human, as well as non-human, others. Some suggest that this works through narrative transport, which is about bringing a reader (or viewer) into a story and seeing through the eyes of the other (Green & Brock, 2000). Animated movies featuring animals as the main protagonists are thought to foster pro-conservation attitudes among children (King, 1996; Whitley, 2008). The movie, *Babe*, was thought to have encouraged a generation of vegetarians, presumably through empathy with the main protagonist (Nobis, 2009).[7]

---

[6] An ability that should not be considered the sole purview of humans, as Jane Goodall reflects on interactions with chimpanzees (Goodall, 1986; see also O'Connell, 1995).

[7] Note, however, that such movies may not always have the intended effect, such as the purported increase in commercial harvest and sale of tropical clownfish after the release of the movie, Finding Nemo, though some have contested this claim (Miltz & Foale, 2017).

Conservationists often tap into this potential, often anthropomorphizing nonhumans to foster empathy for nature (Chan, 2012). Researchers have even found that presenting data in different ways, such as anthropomorphic techniques like using pictograms with human silhouettes instead of symbols, or associating pictures of people with the data, can successfully trigger greater empathy and reveal the people behind the data (Boy et al., 2017). Later in the book, we review evidence suggesting how connectedness promotes empathy and, ultimately, pro-environmental behavior.

The Connected Classroom

The teacher from Pennsylvania, Michael Soskil, recounts the experience of connecting with the classroom in Kibera and singing to each other: "When you have shared emotive experience, you bond with someone. That's how we develop friendships. Singing together was a way of making that happen."

He underscores the fact that the relationship was a mutual one, as relationships are. His students came up with a request from their counterparts in Nairobi:

What they decided to do is ask for the kids in Kibera to teach us Swahili because there is no foreign languages spoken in our hometown … The kids in Kibera would create a YouTube video and they would upload it on the same website teaching us Swahili, and we would play their videos on the morning news broadcast every week where the entire school, K-5, would get learn to count to ten or the months of the year or days of the week in Swahili.

But the exchange went the other way, as well: "The school director (in Kibera) … explained how the water got into the school …which was [through] garden hoses that were duct taped to PVC pipes, and he explained that during the rainy season in April, the pit toilets overflow and sometimes the water supply gets contaminated… so my students collaborated with a group of kids in Andover KS and a group of kids in Trikala, Greece to collaboratively raise money for water filters that would be able to protect the students, teachers and families in Kibera."

And, so, how might we encourage people in the middle of the busy city to care about melting glaciers? One way is through simple, affective connection, according to Soskil. He recounts another story: "I was in the middle of teaching and a teacher friend of mine from Nepal happened to call me on a video conferencing call unexpectedly … I decided to take the call, and I said to my friend 'Look I'm in a middle of lesson here, we're talking about climate change ... do you want to tell us something about climate change in Nepal?' ... I had my students ask him questions and one of them said 'Well you're up on the mountains anyway so climate change isn't affecting you, right?' And he said 'No, what you don't understand is that we are surrounded by glaciers and snow pack and we are having crazy amount of avalanches that are burying whole communities, it more dangerous than ever there.' My students were: 'We never thought of that before!', and it gave them a different perspective just because it was someone at a different place and broke some of their preconceptions that they had."

Connectedness underlies the logic of the social network. Network theorists have begun investigating how coordination and collective action can emerge from the establishment of a network, whether formal or informal. Relationality has not received much treatment in the social network literature, which sees links between nodes in a network in terms of formal ties or material exchange, and not so much in the emergence of empathy between these nodes. The beauty of the network lies in the fact that, while it encompasses a wide reach that touches, say, a thousand people, each person need not be connected to all the other people in the network. It suffices, for a network to be a network, for each person to be connected to even just one other person (as depicted in Figure 1.1). As we will discuss, in some situations, the collective action problem can be solved when a player is linked to just one other player in a large n network. In simpler terms, when we care for one other person, we might find ourselves in a way caring for everybody else in the process. It is a powerful notion, that what some refer to as the "large-n" problem might be solved by just reducing it to something simpler, which is the relationship between two actors: self and other.

In the classic communitarian model, as proposed by Ostrom, a community can establish rules (for resource use or other collective action), monitor individuals, transmit norms, levy sanctions, bestow rewards, and establish reputations. But the logic of relationality can activate cooperation even in the absence of anything resembling an identifiable community. We will see examples of relationality that do not require propinquity or proximity, kinship or homophily, or other things that conventionally bind people into a community. Relationships can work even in the absence of rule-systems, sanctions, and community.

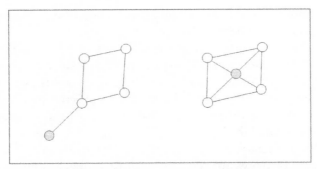

FIGURE 1.1 The singly connected versus multi-connected network actor.

Relationships can even go beyond those among humans. We see countless instances of people developing empathy for nonhuman others (especially when the other is morphologically similar to humans, as with other mammals). For many of the examples of ecological commons that we will be taking up, the ability of relational patterns to extend to non-humans is important.

The modeling of collective action and the commons, from Mancur Olson's to Elinor Ostrom's formulations, has been dominated by the conventional model of individual rationality. Mathematically, this translates to a decision-maker optimizing a utility function with a single variable in its argument, which is the player's own payoff. Game theory involves the construction of hypothetical models to predict human decision-making and behavior. In a game with multiple individually rational decision-makers, John Nash showed that predictable solutions (or equilibria) can be expected for such situations (Nash, 1951). Now, what happens when we model games with other-regarding players, whose decision functions depend on not just the player's own payoff but the others' as well? What outcomes might we find when we model commons situations with a set of players playing a relational logic? Would we find predictable equilibria, as with individually rational players? As we will discuss, it would be interesting to model situations with this slightly more complex notion of human decision-making and to see what different outcomes and patterns of play emerge. Most importantly, we have to try to analyze this type of decision-making, since real people are complex, multiply-motivated decision-makers who care for many things beyond individual payoff. We will take up, in the next chapter, a highly simplified mathematical model of other-regard (as in Lejano & Ingram, 2012), and then in succeeding chapters, turn to richer, qualitative descriptions of relationality.[8]

To be clear, the purpose of the book is not to rehash long-standing critiques of the model of individual rationality or *homo economicus* (e.g., Sen, 1977), but to analyze, for its own worth, the other-regarding side of humanity and explore its implications for collective action. In other words, it is *homo curae* (the caring person), that we turn out attention to. Another idea behind the book is the desire to provide other ways of analyzing collective action, which is dominated by a focus on rational (in the smaller sense of the word) systems of (often formalized but sometimes informal) rules, roles, and organization. We ask: what if the functioning of the system is not to be explained by these elements but, rather, subsists in the relationships, and their functioning, that interconnect the network of policy actors (Lejano, Araral, & Araral, 2014)?

Assumptions about how people make decisions and behave on a micro level lead to institutional designs on a larger scale. The literature has depicted the institutional options for solving collective action problems in a tripartite way. Following Mancur Olson, one can, first, depend on the state to set rules that sanction uncooperative behavior and enforce them, or, secondly, one can look to the market to send economic signals that do the same. Ostrom's third way runs through the community, which acts to set rules, agreed upon by community members, and sanction those who do not play by the rules. This paints the picture with a broad brush – in reality, there are a multitude of competing (sometimes, hybrid) designs. In this book, we examine another way that collective action problems might be solved, which is yet different from the three mentioned mechanisms. We look at the possibility of relationality occurring even outside the bounds of a sanctioning community, and we realize that relational logic works in many ways. In many instances, relationships work in ways that seem to lie outside what one can call rule-systems and community-centered sanctioning of these rules. The ethic of care, as

---

[8] Though it lies outside the scope of this book, there is the challenge of analyzing the nature and action of relationships, which brings us to the problem of defining "relationship." There is some preliminary work in this area – for example, see Lejano (2008) and Lejano and Kan (2022a) where a relationship is modeled as the constitution of one's identity away from the autonomous ego to the three dimensions of: self, self vis-a-vis other, and self-and-other. This establishes the tight connection between relationship and identity. The relational condition is not just a positional concept because it also considers one's joint identity with the other. Moreover, relationship is not just cognitive, and it includes material interactions between self and other, as well. We are reminded that relationships inhere among materially situated selves (Whatmore, 1997).

Carol Gilligan described it (Gilligan, 1993), does not work so much as a deontological rule system – rather, it is an active responsiveness to the other. Yes, people often do good out of adherence to a moral principle, but Gilligan is saying that, oftentimes, people do good not so much in response to an abstract rule but because they have a relationship with another. One route to morality is as valid and important as the other.

The differences between the rule-based and the relational are greater in some contexts – for example, Stone recounts how the transition of elder care from something provided by the family to a professional service involved substituting a system of (countable) rules and routines for the (innumerable) things and attitudes and sentiments involved in caring for a loved one (Stone, 2000). In these instances, it is easy to see how rule systems fail to encompass what it means to care for another. Bourdieu gives a wonderful example of gift-giving among the Kabyle, where trying to capture the institution in a system of rules would defeat the practice of gift-giving, which involves a dynamic relating of one to another in a way not capturable by a rule (Bourdieu, 1977).

To be sure, Ostrom et al. saw beyond communal institutions as simple rule-systems. In her later work, Ostrom began studying how other mechanisms maintained group cooperation, apart from the original model of community-based rules and sanctioning (as simulated by the repeated game). Ostrom and colleagues observed that individually rational behavior emerges from competitive (market) situations that encourage this but found, in other contexts, more complex modes of decision-making: "Actors have preferences related to achieving net benefits for self, but these are combined in many situations with other-regarding preferences and norms about appropriate actions and outcomes that affect their decisions" (Poteete, Janssen, & Ostrom, 2010, 223). In a way, the present book is a continuation of their inquiry into the complex ways people align themselves with the greater good, exploring the phenomenon of relationality, into which Ostrom et al. had begun to inquire.

Should we think of the relational pathway as a "fourth" institutional model? Later in the book, we will examine how relationality can orient members, to collective action, of a social network that may bear no semblance to the communities that Ostrom studied. Some networks are simply agglomerations of individually linked actors and may not have any filial or spatial propinquities that characterize communities – in these cases, we will consider how relationality (through empathy) can coordinate actions throughout such networks. However, as we will discuss, in many situations, relationality is less of an alternative model and more of a parallel process that occurs within conventional institutions. Relationality can occur inside state, market, and communitarian modes of action. Granovetter's example of breadmaking argues that a market is not a market is not a market – that is, each local bread industry differs from the other because each is embedded in a different web of relationships (Granovetter, 1985). Others have described state-centered systems, which are supposed to be impersonal, to often be embedded in relationships as well – for example, what Asian scholars sometimes refer to as guanxi (Xin & Pearce, 1986).

How are we supposed to think about a community that functions more coherently than another due to its greater store of social capital? What is social capital without people learning to care about the other and acting on this? One can think of social organization, within the community, as arising from individually rational logic as one finds in a repeated game. This, however, is like Durkheim trying to separate organic from mechanical solidarity – in real communities, relationality and individual rationality are co-occurrent logics. One can hardly form associations (e.g., joining a community board) without gaining some empathy for, or understanding the perspective of, the other. In some instances, other-regard maybe supported by conditions that combine opportunities for altruism with self-interested behavior (e.g., Mansbridge, 1990).

As we reflect on the power of connectedness, we cannot help but think, too, about the disempowerment that comes from disconnectedness. We find situations where people are most vulnerable who are disconnected from the rest of society. The disaster literature is replete with such stories, such as frail elderly residents living in isolation in the Red Hook apartments in Brooklyn, New York, who went days without help in the aftermath of Superstorm Sandy (Hernandez et al., 2018). During Typhoon Haiyan, many of the victims were informal settlers in the City of Tacloban, Philippines, who lacked institutional ties to government and businesses (Walch, 2018).

The Other Side of the Coin: Vulnerability and Disconnectedness

Dilruba Haider, UN Women's Programme Specialist (DRR, CC, HA) for Bangladesh, addresses a room of government officials and NGOs working on disaster risk reduction in Dhaka. She describes how disasters very often take a greater toll on women. (As an aside, Cyclone

Gorky, in 1991, is said to have wrought more fatalities in Bangladesh among women than men, at a ratio of 14 to 1.*) She hails the recent move toward engagement of community. "This is a good idea, to bring knowledge about risks like tropical cyclones to the marketplace, to the mosque, to the schools." However, she says it is not enough. "But what about many women in Bangladesh, when the women are not to be found in the market, or the mosque, or the schools? How do we reach them, when many do not or cannot even go outside their home? If we want a program that will make change, we have to reach these women who are traditionally excluded from these places and these programs."

* Bern et al. (1993); Lindeboom et al. (2012).

Climate inaction, in the US, was enabled in part by disconnectedness, in the form of climate skeptical communities who were shut off from other perspectives. The alienation of one group from another was ideological, stemming from a climate-skeptical narrative that was closed to other voices and experiences (Lejano & Nero, 2020). The disconnectedness was also regional and cultural, in part, as rural white Americans were markedly opposed to climate action as compared to the urban population (McCright & Dunlap, 2011). Later in the book, we will explore the link between disconnectedness and the more general theme of environmental justice. As we will discuss, environmental injustice can be seen to be rooted in the basic separation from self and other. Relationality can be thought of as two sides of a coin, with connectedness on one side and disconnectedness on the other.

Sometimes, disconnectedness is part of the design of a program. The use of the market as an institutional remedy for collective action problems can alienate people from the other. In the classic market, personal relationships between actors are replaced by impersonal transactions between buyers and sellers through some kind of intermediary exchange. In many instances, a buyer responds to a unitary element of information, which is the price signal, and may not even encounter the person on the other end. Compare this to the complex flesh-and-blood encounter between people in social relationships. Perhaps some of this longing for connectedness lies behind the recent trend toward more personalized encounters in farmers markets, as opposed to the impersonal transactions found in a supermarket (Garner, 2017). We will see examples of retailers who aim to reconnect buyer and producer, such as fair-trade coffee vendors who try to establish some connection between the consumers and the people who grow the coffee.

The book continues a line of questioning that asks: if other-regard, empathy, and altruism are undeniable realities of the human condition, then why do we model human behavior and design institutions as if they were not? In an early investigation of this, a book entitled Beyond Self-Interest, Mansbridge suggests "As empirical social science stops ignoring this reality and starts exploring duty and love with the same intensity it has recently given self-interest, the resulting analyses are likely to become more useful to those engaged in collective action" (Mansbridge, 1990 xiii).

The relational view is about the power of connectedness. To be sure, we don't at all presume that relationships are primarily beneficial. Some relationships, such as those wrought with power differentials, can be unjust for some parties. Relationships can be antagonistic, such as those between people who stay divided in ideologically separated camps. But in these situations, we may find that the ties are not of empathy and that the other might be seen not as a co-equal being but a stick figure, a category, an archetype, or a caricature. Perhaps the other never becomes another being that one can identify with, as people engage in "affective polarization" where stereotypes stand in for the other (Druckman et al., 2022).

Not all interactions foster other-regard. The encounter of a person prone to xenophobia with the foreign other can simply be one of fear and resentment. The hurling of epithets between liberals and conservatives can be like enemies lobbing grenades at each other from their respective trenches. Not all encounters lead to empathy, which leads us to wonder, which interactions do and why do they?

Thinking most broadly, perhaps getting deeper into the prevalence and potential of other-regard can counteract some of the sweeping narcissism that we have seen in our present age. There is an important caveat, however. We formulate a relational model in response to the conventional one that assumes people are simply individually rational. Just as the conventional models leave out too much, we present a relational model without pretending that, at the same time as people think and act in other-regarding ways, they are never *not* individually rational. We note this now because, in succeeding chapters, we will talk about other-regard sometimes in isolation from other motivations that lie within us. This is almost unavoidable when crafting and distilling the essence of a new model. Toward the end of the book, we get back to the reality of how people are, which is utterly complex.[9]

Previewing the rest of the book, readers should feel free to not read the chapters sequentially and are encouraged to jump to sections that engage them directly. For example, a reader may not be so interested in the formal game-theoretic model, discussed in Chapter 2, or the psychological/neurological underpinnings, presented in Chapter 3, as in the role of relationality in promoting pro-social and pro-environmental behavior, as discussed in Chapters 4 and 5. A reader most interested in institutional implications can turn first to Chapter 6. For those with a keen interest in how relationality figures into urgent issues that confront the world at this moment (i.e., the pandemic, racial and social injustice, and climate change), they could turn to Chapter 7.

The succeeding chapters will present the relational model in clearer light, illustrate its use with real-world examples, and work out its potential for institutional reform. The book is meant to be an updating of Ostrom's 1990 classic and, fittingly, will follow its lead at some points. Ostrom's book starts out mathematically, describing the game-theoretic foundations of collective action problems and her nuanced understanding of them. Chapter 2 will establish some of the same foundations, mainly to show how the present concept differs from the established. Games are an effective pedagogical tool for highlighting conceptual points. The point of this book is this: all the outcomes predicted by these toy games, including Ostrom's, turn out differently when we make one change in the formulation, which is to assume decision-makers who base their decisions not just on their own payoffs, but the payoff to the other as well. The chapter will work out how connectivity works for the greater good. Interestingly, for some collective action problems, a decision-maker need not be connected to all those who would be affected by her decision, but it suffices to make a connection with one or two. This is, in part, network logic (since, for most networks of any real consequence, each member is connected to a few, but not all, of the members). The chapter points to the potential of this mathematical model, suggesting what we might obtain once we start modeling economies of other-regarding (instead of simply individually rational) players. Chapter 2 includes some game theory, as did Ostrom's classic book. As with Ostrom's book, the reader who is not particularly interested in

---

[9] One relevant notion is from Berkes, who points out that it is not enough to focus on the cognitive but the knowledge-practice-belief complex (Berkes, 2018).

game-theoretic illustrations is free to skip the chapter and move on to succeeding (non-mathematical) chapters.

The model of the other-regarding person is backed by a considerable store of evidence in different fields of study, which we discuss in Chapter 3. From Husserl to Buber to Levinas, phenomenologists problematized the relationship between self and other and sought to characterize this as a basic (ontological) human condition. Gilligan states it in a fundamental way as an ethic of care. We discuss the psychology literature on altruism, especially the role of empathy in such other-regarding behavior. Within this literature, we find evidence of the role of connectedness in engendering empathy. There are other motivational routes to altruistic behavior (such as reputational effects), and the literature teases out these fine differences. These patterns have evolutionary roots that can be traced to the bond between parent and child, according to some scholars. These insights are backed by a growing body of evidence in neurobiology, which suggests that a stimulus like viewing pictures of a person experiencing pain can trigger an empathic response. These responses are linked to cooperative behavior in experimental games, which simulate collective action in real situations. One important idea emerging from this chapter is that, if theorists of care are right that it is a basic human condition, then relationality and empathy are not simply a "feel-good thing" that one would want to see in the world but cannot rely on. Relationality is more than this, since it is constitutive of who we are.

In Chapter 4, we examine evidence for the relational thesis in real-world examples of pro-social and pro-environmental behavior. Charity foundations and aid organizations have learned that providing some kind of connection between potential donor and recipient, whether it consists of pictures or bios or direct connection, increases people's willingness to help. The role of empathy in gift giving has been explored in some of this literature. We see supporting evidence in pro-social consumerism, such as people's willingness to pay extra for fair trade coffee. Accordingly, fair trade organizations have begun making the farmers and other beneficiaries at the supply end more tangible to consumers.

Chapter 5 takes up examples of the commons. Ostrom's theory of common-pool resources has been influential in many areas such as water resource management and habitat conservation. Some examples in these areas, however, suggest the commons are being sustained without the system of rules-in-place and community-based feedback mechanisms suggested by Ostrom's theory. Several real-world cases are described.

In one example from habitat conservation, actual practices deviated, in nonsimplistic ways, from formal rules in a way that cohered to the relationships the conservationists had with the community. In case studies on water resource management, involving co-determination of use policies, we will see how the participatory forums worked to allow hitherto disconnected players to develop an understanding of the perspectives, feelings, hopes, and aspirations of the other. Their design is related to principles emerging from the relational theory, such as the need to increase connectedness, to build recognition of the other, and to increase transparency of the system. This leads to Chapter 6, which focuses on institutional design.

Focusing on relationality and the consequences of connectedness leads to principles for designing institutions, which is taken up in Chapter 6. The idea is that fostering connections between individuals and groups increases mutual identification, which triggers a sense of care. Information-based strategies for environmental (and other) regulation can be guided by these principles, including that of building into the institution connections with those being affected or helped by the action. These connectivities can take advantage of new media that allow direct access to the images, voice, and face-to-face contact from the field. The idea of fair-trade coffee outlets giving buyers access (whether direct or indirect) to the families that grow the coffee is an example of this. Many of the design principles have to do with building social networks and allowing deeper and sustained relationships across boundaries, bringing together those who normally would be disconnected. The principles also embody many tenets of the ethical theory of care, such as ensuring that the most vulnerable are connected and cared for, that the voiceless are heard, and that norms for the equitable treatment of all are emphasized. In the design of governance arrangements for the commons, relational principles complement those for common-pool resources and are not an alternative to them. In form, relational strategies stand in contrast to Ostrom's – for example, while common-pool resource theory emphasizes the need to establish formal boundaries, the relational theory aims to bridge these boundaries and increase connectedness. While Ostrom's design principles emphasize systems of rules, relationality emphasizes connectedness and caring. As the pendulum of institutional theory swings from state to market to community (and all regions in between), we consider whether relationality in social networks might be considered a "fourth way" or, rather, as something immanent in all of these models.

Chapter 7, the concluding chapter, takes a broader look at the human condition and reflects on the relevance of the relational perspective. We revisit the central ideas of the book and apply them to a specific example, that of climate change mitigation. We then look at the intersection of relationality with other important themes, including environmental justice, sustainability, and resilience. Relational ways of coping with global crises require that people discover, re-discover, and nurture the bonds that help one connect with the other. On the contrary, disconnectedness and treatment of persons as impersonal others results in a spectrum of conditions, from everyday microaggressions to systematic injustice.

Directions for future work are discussed in this concluding chapter. This includes the need to work out how the relational mechanism interacts with other behavioral mechanisms identified by Ostrom, Olson, and others. When does the relational mechanism take over and dominate that of individual rationality, and vice-versa? How do we craft institutions that take advantage of all three models? There is an open question that pertains to institutional models. While Olson's work suggested a choice between state-centered and market-centered institutional models, a multitude of (hybrid) designs work by increasing interaction between multiple actors in network governance arrangements (e.g., Mulgan, 2012 and Lejano, 2020). The chapter sketches some research ideas to be explored in the coming years, such as how to create institutions that increase connectedness between people who are not ordinarily part of the same social network? How can digital media be used to connect hitherto disconnected groups, perhaps even making the specter of melting glaciers salient to those in the cosmopolitan city? What are the implications for environmental communication and education? How might we go about reconnecting people who have taken up polarized ideological positions? And, lastly, what are some directions for scholars of collective action?

This book constitutes a small but significant step toward a concerted research program revolving around relationality. Its main theme is about restoring connections between the hitherto disconnected, allowing the family of living beings to learn to again care for each other.

The book should be seen not so much as a rejoinder to Ostrom's classic text but an addendum. The idea of relationality lies embedded in the work of Ostrom and her colleagues, but it has not been examined in a deep way. Relationality needs to be considered as a crucial component of the concerted effort at solving problems of the commons. In fact, some dilemmas may not be amenable to other institutional remedies and may require, whatever the solution is, the fostering of empathy for the other. Why and how else would the busy urbanite do anything for stranded polar bears or unfairly paid coffee plantation workers? To regulate or price in solutions to these kinds of issues maybe too daunting a task or might spur protest among those who already feel put upon by the market and the state (and elites). Connecting each of us to one another builds on a natural human condition and creates a motivational pathway that needs to be fully explored. This is an important point. As we will develop in this book, relationality is not just about solving problems – even more than this, it is about being our most authentic selves.

2

Constructing a Relational Theory
of Collective Action

In Governing the Commons, Elinor Ostrom began by recalling the classic prisoner's dilemma of early game theory (first discussed in Flood et al., 1950). Scholars often use this kind of pedagogic strategy (of constructing simplified games) to clarify the concept being illustrated. To be sure, these "toy games" do not come close to representing the complexities of real-world situations and the decision-making of real people, but they highlight key concepts in effective and sensible ways. We will do the same in this chapter, mostly to frame the relationality thesis in a clear and simple way, without suggesting that the model presented herein can represent the phenomena of connectedness in its complexity. A reader not interested in game theory can skip this mathematical treatment and move onto the next and subsequent chapters, which looks at other evidence of relationality, both in the lab and the real world.

We can begin, as Ostrom did, by depicting the game with the example of herders raising cows on a common pasture. The pasture is owned by no one and freely accessible to all, hence the term, the commons. In the terms used in political economy, free access means that the resource is non-excludable. However, use of the pasture by one herder interferes with its use by another herder. Their cows can bump into each other, compete for grass and shade, and create other externalities, so the resource is what is known as a rival good. The example will be well-known to many readers, so we will not belabor all the details. The point is that there is a sustainable number of cows raised on the pasture which ensures a maximum return to all the herders. For simplicity's sake, assume everything is symmetrical across the herders, so the ideal situation is that each herder raises the same "responsible" number of cows.

The problem is that, acting alone, each herder will raise more than the responsible number of cows, leading to the ruin of the pasture, with the result that everybody loses and earns less revenue than they could have had. The tragedy is that they all know that raising too many cows would result in such ruin. Yet, the inexorable logic of self-interest leads each to act irresponsibly. Hardin would refer to this dilemma as the tragedy of the commons (Hardin, 1968).

Why does the informed but self-interest-seeking herder act irresponsibly, even while fully knowing about the tragedy of the commons game? The logic goes something like this: each herder considers cooperating but realizes: "If the other(s) act uncooperatively, I will be even worse off and the only one ruined – ergo, I would minimize my losses if I acted uncooperatively, too." As the tragic story goes, everyone reasons the same way, acts noncooperatively, and the pasture is ruined. A general term for this type of dilemma is the collective action problem, due to Mancur Olson (1965). How is the dilemma solved? In either of two ways, Olson reasoned. Either the pasture is privatized and fenced off, with each herder getting their respective plots, or the state steps in and regulates how many cows each herder can put out to pasture. Either strategy, privatization, or regulation, will incentivize (or coerce) each herder to limit their cows to the sustainable number.

Ostrom's keen insight was to claim that there is a third way to solve the dilemma: not market, not government, but community (Ostrom, 1987). Community can exert social pressure on uncooperative individuals in order to nudge them toward better behavior. The key, Ostrom continued, is to rethink the commons game as not something that is played once but played repeatedly, such that cooperative behavior, or sanctions against uncooperative behavior, can evolve over time. The game-theoretic basis for this lies in the so-called Folk theorem, which states that cooperative results in the prisoner's dilemma (and other similar) games can be achieved in a repeated (not one-shot) game situation where a strategy for incentives and sanctions can be applied by players on the uncooperative one.[1] One such strategy is known as tit-for-tat where, in a two-player situation, player A plays uncooperatively in the second round if player B is uncooperative in the first round, and plays cooperatively if the other cooperated previously (Rapoport, 1974). The logic is that each player realizes: if I don't cooperate now, the other(s) will make me pay

---

[1] Proof of the Folk Theorem is due to Aumann and Shapley (1976), as well as Rubinstein (1979).

for this in the future, so best I cooperate. In a one-shot game, a player can just choose not to cooperate and walk away, not having to interact with the other players again. However, a repeated game requires longer-term thinking.

For this chapter's purposes, the key idea is that Ostrom's community-based logic, as originally stated, is still consistent with the notion of individual rationality, which is that of the decision-maker maximizing her/his own payoff. Note that, as we will discuss in succeeding chapters, Ostrom's own later work can be understood as going beyond this utilitarian model, as well. Nonetheless, the basic logic of the model she presented derived from the logic of the repeated game.

Where this book begins is where the repeated game formulation leaves off. What if, we ask, community members not only interact repeatedly (thus, allowing monitoring and sanction) but, in fact, also develop connections (particularly personal connections) among themselves? What if such connectedness fosters other-regard and, in fact, empathy for the other? The key difference that we will discuss in this chapter is that we not only conceptualize a player's decision as that which optimizes her or his own payoff but as something that includes consideration for the other's payoff (or payoffs) as well. To show how this matters, let us represent the situation in mathematical form. We introduce the following variables.

Let us imagine a pasture with three herders or players (i, j, and k).

X_i = the number of cows that player i decides to raise,

p_i = the payoff from the game to player i,

$\sum p$ = sum of players' payoffs, $p_i + p_j + p_k$,

$u_i(p_i, p_j, p_k)$ = utility to player i from the combination of payoffs (p_i, p_j, p_k).

A player's payoff is a function of the number of cows she decides to raise. Just for example's sake, let us use a well-behaved (concave) function like the following and assume this holds for every player:

$$p_i = 60\, x_i - x_i 2 - \left[x_j^2 + x_k^2 \right]$$

where the expression in the brackets is the externality or costs imposed upon player i by the other's activity.

Let us start with the conventional assumption that players are individual rational. As the logic of the tragedy of the commons goes, when player i maximizes his individual return, his calculation proceeds are follows:

max p_i which means $\partial p_i / \partial x_i = 60x_i - x_i^2 = 0$

which leads to a solution of $x_i = 30$ (meaning, player i raises thirty cows)

However, we quickly realize that were each player to use the same reasoning, the pasture would go to ruin and everybody would wind up at a loss. Since we assumed the game was symmetrical, we have everybody raising thirty cows each, resulting in the following payoff to each person.

Uncooperative strategy $p = 60(30) - 302 - (302 + 302) = -900$ (i.e., a negative result for everyone).

This is a far cry from what they could earn were each player to raise a more sustainable number of cows, which we determine from the calculation shown below.

$$\Sigma p = p_i + p_j + p_k = 180x - 9x^2$$

Differentiating both sides, we have $\partial \Sigma p / \partial x = 180 - 18x$ which leads to an ideal solution of $x = 10$ (i.e., ten cows each).

We see the merit of the cooperative approach by calculating the resulting payoff to each player.

Cooperative strategy $p = 60(10) - 3(102) = 300$ (i.e., a positive result for everyone).

As the narrative goes, the tragedy of the commons is that each player could wind up so much better off, earning 300, by cooperating, but they all end up not cooperating (by putting out too many cows) and losing 900 as a result.

Why does each player decide not to cooperate? Because they realize that, if they do cooperate and others don't, they lose even more, winding up with a net return of −1,020 (the readers can verify this calculation on their own).

Here we introduce relationality. What if, somehow, the players were each connected and felt an empathy for the other? Mathematically, their decision functions would not simply be to maximize their individual payoffs but something that involves consideration of the other's payoff, as well. Many possible functions found in the literature can account for other-regard. For this chapter, we will assume a simple one, which is the maximin function, shown below. This function simply has a player comparing her payoff with the other's and making a decision that maximizes the payoff of whoever has the lowest return. In philosophical ethics, this might correspond to Rawl's so-called difference principle which prescribes that decision that results in the greatest good for the least advantaged (Rawls, 1971).

maximin rule: $u_i(p_i, p_j, p_k) = \max\left[\min(p_i, p_j, p_k)\right]$

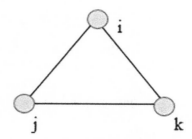

FIGURE 2.1 Example of a social network.

and, since we assumed the game is symmetrical, our solution simply equates all three:

$p_i = p_j = p_k$

and the decision-maker realizes that the maximum result achieved that also equates all player's payoffs is simply the ideal cooperative result (i.e., ten cows each).

We can diagram connectedness as a social network (as shown in Figure 2.1) where each player is connected to the other.

If the reader is all right with this logic thus far, we will press on. Those who want to read up on the evidentiary basis for other-regard and decision-making that exhibits empathy and egalitarianism might want to take a quick look at the topics covered in the succeeding chapter. There is ample evidence, from fields such as psychology and neurobiology, of other-regard as an active mode of reasoning (and being).

At this point, we take up the "small n" problem. That is, if indeed connectedness can foster other-regard, how can this be achieved in a situation with many actors who cannot each be personally connected with every other actor in the network? This is especially true if one insists on direct interpersonal contact. We can respond in at least three ways. The first is to point out that, depending on the structure of the game and the decision functions, sometimes, merely being cognizant of the welfare of just one other person (or a few other persons) can prime a person to act for the whole. Take the situation depicted above and suppose that two persons were connected to only one other centrally-located person in the three-person group (depicted as shown in Figure 2.2).

In the network depicted in Figure 2.2, consider the decision process of player *i* who, being connected only to player *j*, perhaps does not know about (or disregards) player *k*. His maximin function is as follows (player *i* assumes *j* is cooperative and raises ten cows).

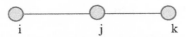

i   j   k

FIGURE 2.2 "Linear" social network diagram.

$$\max\left[\min\left(p_i, p_j\right)\right] = \max\left[\min\left(60x_i - x_i^2 - 100,\ 600 - 100 - x_i^2\right)\right]$$

and, equating the two expressions/payoffs, we get the same cooperative result as before, where $x_i = 10$. So, in this particular example, we see that merely being cognizant of one other player's welfare, a player is moved to act for the good of the whole network. Note that we would not always get such a perfect result. If readers wish to try, they can tweak the decision functions and see that, depending on what specific parameters they choose, they might obtain results in between the cooperative and uncooperative solutions.

The second way we might address the small n issue is to point out, as will be discussed in the next chapter, that relationality can act in much more varied and complex ways than we cover in our simple mathematical example above. It is possible that one's contact with another's plight moves the person to empathize with an entire group of vulnerable individuals and act accordingly. Or, perhaps encountering the other triggers a commitment toward a higher moral plane, which results in altruistic actions that go beyond the payoff-driven logic we discussed above. Kahneman et al., (1999) put it in a slightly different way, which is that, often, a person's attitudes toward a large group are not influenced much by group size because they are determined by one's attitudes toward a representative member of the group.

The third way to address the issue is to consider that there will undoubtedly be situations where the small n problem is a serious obstacle and that other solutions are needed. Perhaps in some situations, connectedness works well for tens or hundreds, but not thousands, of people. Or, as we point out in Chapter 6 on institutions, in reality, different routes toward cooperative behavior are not mutually exclusive, and that measures aimed at connecting people can be taken at the same time as other strategies (e.g., market incentives, along with relationship-building). As an example of the simultaneity of different mechanisms, Mansbridge points out how an Ostrom-like set of community-imposed sanctions against defection can create an ecological niche, wherein altruistic agents are protected against being punished for their cooperative inclinations and, so, are free to act upon their tendencies toward other-regard (Mansbridge, 1990).

2.1 FORMAL THEORY

In decision-theoretic terms, relationality is generally stated as the condition wherein one's decision function includes the payoffs or utilities of the other(s). This allows any number of different modes of decision-making, ranging in degrees from egoistic to altruistic.

A more formal treatment of the above model is found in the Addendum at the end of this chapter. This provides the decision-theorist or political economist with a more explicitly mathematical treatment of the model, which revolves around the existence of Nash equilibria in games with vector payoffs. The Addendum discusses theoretical implications (which are not the main focus of this book), namely, how would acknowledging other-regard in individual decision-making affect the way economic situations are modeled, and what differences in expected outcomes might be expected? This slightly more complex formulation of the decision-maker brings the models a little closer to the real world.

2.2 EXPERIMENTAL GAMES

Just as, for the most part, economists and other researchers had assumed, out of faith, that human behavior would be adequately modeled with the decision-theoretic formulation of the individually rational person, we could just as easily assume that the model of the other-regarding individual might be something self-evident. However, an even better route is to start testing some of these assumptions. Over the last thirty years, researchers have begun to test some of the propositions of these game-theoretic models in the lab.

Researchers began simulating these decision situations, very often with college students. One renowned experiment, known as the ultimatum game, goes as follows. A player (A) is asked to propose a split of some sum of money (e.g., $100) between self and another person. Most often, the identity of the other person is unknown, and the two participants never get to see or hear each other. Player B is then given A's proposed split (e.g., $60 to self, and $40 to B), and B decides to accept or reject it. If B accepts, then they each get the stipulated split of the money, and if B rejects, they both get zero. Assuming that A is an individually rational decision-maker (meaning, a person who tries to maximize one's own payoff) and, knowing that B is likewise the same, what would A offer B? The reader can think through this thought experiment and figure out some answer (which is given in the footnote below).[2]

An even simpler version of this, called the dictator game, only involves the first stage, where A proposes some split of the money. B does not even get a chance to consider the offer and is relegated to simply accepting what A decides. What would you predict the outcome of this game to be, again assuming that both players are utility maximizers (also in the footnote below)?

The interesting thing about these games is that, the more researchers tried them out, the more they noticed that, very often, results departed from the predicted outcomes of these games. Participants would offer the other amounts much larger than that predicted and, often, would even offer a 50–50 split. (A few would even give away the entire 100). Most generally, offers would range between close to zero and a 50–50 split. These deviant outcomes were obtained so often that some researchers called them anomalies and began to go about trying to explain them (e.g., Camerer and Thaler, 1995).

There are many possible reasons that outcomes might deviate from the self-utility maximizing result. Perhaps the offering player was wary of effects on reputation, creating some negative image of him or herself (e.g., Mifune et al., 2010) or that the researcher carrying out the procedure with the participants might form a negative moral judgment (Levitt and List, 2007). Yet, as much as researchers tried to correct for these conditions, the anomalous outcomes persisted.

To many of these investigators, the (tentative) conclusion was that humans exhibit some type(s) of other-regarding criteria in their decision-making. This is not to say that these explanations were uniform, as different players exhibit different norms and other-regarding motivations. Some proposed that people were driven by considerations of equity, which can show up as a desire to minimize the differences in utility received by different people – essentially wanting to avoid unjust rewards, envy, and other comparative considerations (e.g., Rabin, 1993, Bolton & Ockenfels, 2000, and Fehr & Schmidt, 2006). Some attributed generosity in these games to the "warm-glow" of giving – that is, people

---

[2] The conventional solution (or, Nash equilibrium) to the ultimatum game is that A offers as small an amount of money as possible to B (sometimes labeled epsilon, ε, representing some amount close to zero, like one cent), which B then accepts. (Question for students: Why would B accept some amount very close to zero?) As for the dictator game, the solution is that A simply keeps all the money.

feel good about donating goods to others (e.g., Andreoni, 1990). Some propose that, even in situations where repeated play is not allowed, players innately maintain a sense of reciprocity (e.g., Gouldner, 1960). Others attributed the anomaly to social learning, specifically, the diffusion of social norms about giving (e.g., Grossman & Eckel, 2015). We should be open to all these different motivations and consider these as possible mechanisms for generosity (and they each probably do occur in the real world). Not all of them equate with the particular notion of other-regard that we study in this book, which is how people might develop empathy from connectedness, but all of them surely overlap in some fashion.

This experimental work led to many interesting conjectures, backed up with some evidence in the lab and, to some extent, the field. The degree of generosity, as might be expected, varies greatly depending on the circumstances of the experiment and the identities, social positions, and backgrounds of the participants. Gender maybe a relevant variable, as some research has suggested that females tend toward greater generosity or other-regard than males (e.g., Andreoni & Vesterlund, 1997; Eckel & Grossman, 1998) while others found no significant difference (e.g., Bolton & Katok, 1995). Political ideology can be another determinant (e.g., Dawes, Loewn, & Fowler, 2011). A group of researchers, employing the ultimatum and dictator games in the field, obtained findings suggesting that different cultures, across regions and nations, had varying tendencies toward other-regard (e.g., Henrich et al., 2004). Another group conducted cross-country comparisons of outcomes in the dictator game and obtained findings suggesting that people in more developed economies tend to make lower offers in the game (Cochard et al., 2021). But, invariably, all find evidence of some departure from strict individual rationality.

Some researchers found that generosity seems to increase with decreasing "social distance," where social distance is gauged by degree of social or physical propinquity. One explanation for this effect is that perhaps lesser social distance is associated with a sense of heightened reciprocity (e.g., Hoffman et al., 1996). Other researchers attribute the effect to a sense of connectedness, echoing propositions forwarded in this book. Bohnet and Frey designed a test that compared reciprocity and connectedness as possible explanations and demonstrated that connectedness had the greater effect, commenting that "When social distance decreases, the 'other' is no longer some unknown individual from some anonymous crowd but becomes an "identifiable victim" (Bohnet and Frey, 1999, 335).

TABLE 2.1 *Wilcoxon (paired sample) signed-rank test results.*

Amount given to anonymous person	Amount given to identifiable person	Z	p
146.0	193.9	−2.61	0.009[*]

[*] significant to greater than 95 percent level of confidence, paired sample $n = 25$ (*Source: Lejano, 2023*).

In the rest of this section, we illustrate how we can use these experimental games to test various hypotheses regarding connectedness and giving. For example, to what extent is identifiability, mentioned in the previous paragraph, a trigger for other-regarding behavior? In a modified dictator game, the author asked players to divide up an amount (Pesos 400) between self and other. Two groups were tested, each with twenty-five players: a control group where the recipient of the donation was completely anonymous, and a second group where the recipient was named (but not personally known to the decision-maker). The results, summarized in Table 2.1, show that players in the second group (with the identifiable recipient) tended to give significantly more (an average of about forty-eight units more) than the control group, lending credence to the notion that connectedness (at least the form tested herein) can lead to other-regard and altruism. In other words, simply knowing that the "other" is a specific individual (as opposed to a nameless anonymity) can trigger other-regard. This finding supports the literature on the increased importance that people give to the "identifiable victim" (e.g., Schelling, 1968).

In another variation of this game, the decision-maker was asked to first split the 400 between self and a "green climate fund." There were no details given for the fund, apart from the name and information that it was a fund to support carbon mitigation projects around the world. The players were then asked to play the game a second time, with the difference that this time around, three specific projects that could be supported within the green climate fund. The three projects were described, with pictures attached: (a) a solar energy farm (the picture showing a hand pointing to a solar device), (b) a wind turbine project (the picture showing a man holding a small portable turbine), and (c) a reforestation project (the picture showing a group of young children playing around the trees). The experiment tests whether giving to the fund increases when, first, the recipient projects are more tangible and visualizable and,

TABLE 2.2 *Results of GCF donation game (n = 35).*

Increase in amount donated to GCF	Amounts donated to specific GCF projects		
	Solar energy	Wind turbine	Reforestation
267.3*	87.4	85.5	129.4
		302.3*	

* Difference between means significant to greater than 95 percent confidence (paired sample, $n = 35$).

secondly, whether donations increase with the level of human presence in the pictures (with the presence of humans increasing from a to b to c). The results are shown in Table 2.2.

In this experiment, identifiability is attempted not by giving names but showing faces. The first hypothesis seems to have been borne out, which is that people may tend to donate more (by thirty-five units) when the recipient project is identifiable. But, secondly, the results (which show people giving the most to the reforestation project by a significant margin) tend to support the idea that, perhaps, people feel a greater connection to the project that shows a group of children at the project site. There was no increase in giving to the turbine project compared to the solar project, even though the turbine graphic showed a picture with a man's face. Perhaps empathy increases not only with the greater number of people in the reforestation picture but even more so because the pictures showed children. The results are are merely suggestive, since there are other possible ways to explain the results (e.g., perhaps the respondents just find reforestation more attractive than solar energy and wind energy projects).

2.3 RELATIONAL GOODS AND RELATIONAL CAPITAL

The collective action problem is framed as a situation involving a public good (or public bad). A public good is, by definition, non-excludable, which means that, once provided, no one can be prevented from enjoying it. It is also non-rival, which means that one person's consumption of the good does not decrease another's consumption of it. For example, reducing one's use of energy creates a public good, in terms of climate change, since the reduction of carbon emissions benefits everyone (non-excludable) and one's benefit does not reduce another's (non-rival).

Charitable giving for environmental causes can constitute a public good – for example, donating to a climate action fund or donating to bank a hectare of tropical forest and prevent clear-cutting.

Recall, too, Ostrom's notion of a common-pool resource, which is non-excludable but rivalrous. When no boundaries or access rights are in place, then anyone can have access to the resource. One person's consumption of the resource reduces another's. Bananas on a tree growing wild on public land is an example of this. In this and subsequent chapters, we make the case that relationality is relevant to both the public good and common-pool resource situations.

In the light of the discussion above on relationality, the donation example suggests another kind of good. One can choose to donate to specific recipients. The donation to a specific individual would not constitute a non-excludable good because the good is allocable only to the chosen recipient. It is rival because the donated funds cannot be used by another recipient. But, in a very local sense, there is a degree of publicness to the transaction because, in relational terms, not just the recipient benefits, but the giver as well (as opposed to a purely private good that would benefit only the recipient). The good creates benefits for the giver when it is shared or given away. In another sense, this type of good is only activated when shared. We might refer to this as a *relational good*, which provides benefits only when shared between connected individuals. It might be thought of as a kind of public good in a local sense, where publicness only holds in that space encompassing the individuals involved. A relational good might be defined as a good (or benefit) that is created among directly connected members of a social network whenever there is an exchange between them. Such exchange leads to an increase in utility experienced by the recipient of an altruistic act as well as the one performing it.

The sociological literature employs another concept of a kind of good that has proven to be useful in the literature on collective action, and this is the idea of social capital. Bourdieu (1977) describes social capital as a kind of investment or resource that involves an underlying reciprocity. If one person does a good for another, or gives another a certain amount of good, then it is like banking capital that, someday in the future, the recipient will pay back and do the original giver a favor in return. In some respects, a relational act, originating from a condition of altruism, is not like banking, since the act of giving immediately redounds back to the giver. There is no need for reciprocity at a future time. This suggests that we might think of this type of resource as a kind of *relational capital*, which benefits all those involved just by virtue of something being shared (like the covalent bond between two hydrogens). If there is anything banked, it could in some cases be the relationship itself, which might be triggered anytime in the future as a conduit for resource sharing.

2.4 A NOTE ON INSTITUTIONAL IMPLICATIONS

Embedded in the simple games used in the political economy literature are some institutional issues that we will discuss in depth in Chapters 5 and 6. But, even at this early point, we have some foreshadowing of discussions to come. Often unnoticed in many discussions of the prisoner's dilemma game is the presumption that its players are disconnected. They cannot communicate or forge any understanding between them. Our theory begins when we allow connection, even relationship, among these actors.

Also, in Chapters 5 and 6, we will have an opportunity to appreciate Ostrom's later work, which did acknowledge the complexity of human decision-making, including the power of relationship-building. Invariably, some of its early foundations in the logic of the repeated game have an influence on the elements of the institutional theory that she and colleagues built up. There is a strong focus on rules (including implicit or informal rules), monitoring, and mutual sanctioning (done through community mechanisms). As we will discuss, rules and sanctions are part of any institution, including the ones we will be highlighting, but empathy through connectedness can have a distinct or additional effect. As already mentioned, each of the different institutional models often occur in conjunction with others in real practice. Our theory and model puts a spotlight on different institutional mechanisms that can work apart from systems of rules and sanctions. Our focus is on the potential for collective action through connectedness, its underlying logic not based primarily on redirecting individually rational behavior toward the collective good but on inserting into individual decision-making a regard for the welfare of the other. Institutions are needed to foster connectedness, network-building, and interpersonal exchange. We will discuss these matters, as well as our model's implications for social network theory, in Chapter 6.

2.5 PRELUDE

Two important points should be noted. The first pertains to the question of whether, in fact, there is other evidence (outside the experimental game research cited in this chapter) that people do think and decide in other-regarding ways. Or, are we simply just assuming that people have empathy for others? Whenever scholars bring up this question, one is moved to ask, why was this sort of inquiry not done vis-a-vis the assumption of individual rationality? The idea that people are, en toto, utility maximizers, has been the foundation for neoclassical economics and an assumption largely assumed to be a given. Nevertheless, in the next chapter, we will discuss evidence, from fields such as psychology and neurobiology, that people do, in fact, systematically think and decide in other-regarding ways (and, by the way, also in individually rational ways). In Chapter 3, we will look at real-world examples of other-regard at work.

The second point is that the mathematical treatments are, by and large, simplified models of human cognition and decision-making. They are simplified models because these allow us to deduce clear patterns of behavior that help us understand real-world phenomena. Scholars make use of the prisoner's dilemma model because of its outstanding pedagogic qualities. In reality, no serious social scientist will insist that actual human reasoning is so neatly captured by these elemental models. The reality is far more complex (e.g., Mansbridge, 1990; Sober & Wilson, 1999; Enfield & Levinson, 2006; Van Lange et al., 2007). We will go beyond the simple model, in the next and succeeding chapters, and deepen what we mean by relationality.

Relationality is not simply (and not even proximally) a "feel good" thing that one hopes will happen with people but cannot assume to be a realistic option for solving world problems. As we will discuss, it is, in fact, part of the way that people actually are. It is also a mechanism that can be facilitated, in systematic ways, but this requires institutional designs that do so, a prelude to succeeding chapters. Readers who are not interested in the mathematical formulation of the relational model can skip the following Addendum and move ahead to Chapter 3, which discusses psychological and other evidence for empathy and connectedness.

2.6 CHAPTER ADDENDUM

This section is for those with an interest in the mathematical basis of the game-theoretic models discussed above, including the prisoner's dilemma game and the change that comes about when decision-makers take into account the welfare of the other. It appears as an appendix because it is not a necessary part of the book but of enough interest for some that it should be included.

One common point of interest for theorists is the question of whether we can be assured, or not, of the existence of solutions to these games. By "solution", what is meant are so-called equilibria where each player makes assumptions about what other player's utility-maximizing strategies are and adjusts their own maximizing strategy accordingly. If each player's guesses about what other player's strategies are, are indeed the actual strategies other play, then this is a predictable solution to the game. It is called an equilibrium because, since each player is already playing their optimal strategy, there is no incentive for anyone to change their strategy (e.g., how many cows to send out to pasture). It would be eventually known as the Nash equilibrium after John Nash who provided a general proof of existence of these equilibria for a general class of n-person games (Nash, 1950).

In the reference noted above, Nash proved the existence of predictable, equilibrium solutions for noncooperative games (such as the prisoner's dilemma) where each player seeks to maximize their own individual utility (i.e., individually rational players). The question for us is what happens when we slightly modify the decision functions so that they are a function not just of the player's utility but other players" utilities, as well? Would we find Nash equilibria, and what outcomes would we find in these games?

Previous work has laid the foundations for the other-regarding model (details found in Lejano, 2023). Mathematical notation is as follows.

$N = \{1,...,n\}$ is the set of players.

S_i is the strategy space for players i and, for this case, is a subset of $\mathbb{R}$.

$S = S_1 \times S_2 \times ... \times S_n$ is the strategy space for the n-player game and is the Cartesian product of the individual strategy spaces.

$s_i \in S_i$ is a particular strategy of player i

$v_i : S \to \mathbb{R}$ is the payoff function for player i

$v_i(s) = p_i$ is the payoff to i for strategy n-tuple $s \in S$

$v(s) = \{v_1(s),...,v_n(s)\} = (p_1,...,p_n) \in \mathbb{R}^n$ is the payoff function for the game for $s \in S$

$P =$ payoff space for the game.

$U =$ utility space for the game.

$u_i : P \to \mathbb{R}$ is the utility function for player i

$u_i(p) = u_i$ is the utility for i for payoff n-tuple $p \in P$.

$u_i(p) = \{u_i(p),...,u_n(p)\} = (u_1,...,u_n)$ is the utility function for the game for $p \in P$.

$s \setminus t_i$ denotes $(s_1,...,s_{i-1},t_i,s_{i+1},...,s_n)$ or the combination strategy, s, with t_i substituted for s_i.

$p \setminus q_i$ denotes $\left(p_1,...,p_{q-1},q_i,p_{i+1},...,p_n\right)$ or the payoff vector, p, with q_i substituted for p_i.

Instead of merely maximizing v_i, player i's best response involves maximizing the composite function, $(u \circ v)_i$, as shown below.

$(u \circ v)_i : S \to \mathbb{R}$ is the composition of u_i and v_i.

$(u \circ v)(s) = \{u_1(p),...,u_n(p)\} = \{u_1(v(s)),...,u_n(v(s))\}$ where $v(s) = p \in \mathbb{R}^n$, $s \in S$.

The best-reply mapping $r_i : S \to S_i$ for i is a correspondence associating each strategy combination $s \in S$ with a subset of S_i such that $r_i(s) = \{t_i \in S_i \mid (u \circ v)_i(s \setminus t_i) = max_{s_i \in S_i}(u \circ v)_i(s \setminus s_i)\}$

The best-reply mapping, $r : S \to S$, is a correspondence associating each strategy combination $s \in S$ with a subset of S where $r(s)$ is the Cartesian product of individual best-responses that is, $r(s) = r_1(s) \times r_2(s) \times ... \times r_n(s)$

The key difference with the other-regarding model is that there are two functions to consider. The first, v_i, is the same as the Nash formulation – it is the vector of payoffs that each player gets from playing the game. But the decision in our model arises from another function, u_i, which is player i's decision function, which depends on not just i's own payoff, but the payoff of the other players, as well. As is required in these proofs, sufficient conditions are prescribed for these functions, as follows.

The rest of the proof entails showing that other-regarding players can reach an equilibrium set of strategies, where each player has a utility function that includes the payoffs for the other players and, moreover, employs a strategy that maximizes this utility function. Moreover, this optimal strategy is based on assumptions regarding the other players" respective strategies and, at the equilibrium, these assumptions correctly match what the other player's respective optimal strategies are.

One conventional way of showing this is to prove that the game has a fixed point. First, one makes the standard assumption that S_i is compact and convex for each $i \in N$, $S_i \in \mathbb{R}$, along with various assumed properties (continuity, concavity) in the utility and payoff functions.

As was previously defined, $r(s)$ is a correspondence, the domain of which, S, is compact and convex. The proof then proceeds by showing that r has a fixed point, $\left(\text{i.e., there exists some } s^* \in S \text{ for which } s^* \in r(s^*)\right)$. Using the notation, Γ, where $\Gamma = (N, S, P, v, u)$, represent the noncooperative game of complete information, then the proof assures us that Γ has at least one Nash equilibrium (Lejano, 2023).

The implication is that decision-makers with other-regarding preferences can expect to find equilibrium solutions in these game situations, much like games modeled with individually rational players. This means that, in games with complete information, players with other-regarding preference structures can predict how other other-regarding players would play and optimize their strategies accordingly. With each player following their optimal strategies, we can find predictable equilibrium solutions to the game. Essentially, this gives us some positive indication that, so long as we can even roughly understand how people combine preferences for their individual payoff with preferences for the others" payoffs, then we can reasonably model these games as with classic individually rational players.

3

Further Justifications of the Relational Theory

In this chapter, we further our exploration of what it means to be relational. In what ways does relationality define us, and what evidence exists to support this representation of the human condition? As will be discussed, some research from fields such as social psychology and neurobiology supports the contention that connectedness fosters empathy. We also examine how conditions in the modern world act against relationality.

As endearingly depicted in Antoine de Saint-Exupéry's The Little Prince, a relationship is like seeing the one rose as unique among the hundreds of thousands of other roses. Having tamed the fox, the prince saw it as his fox, unique in all the world, not simply one of a species. Having tamed the other (in other words, having nurtured a relationship), you are forever responsible for the other. What an ethic this would be for a world in perpetual ecological destruction – that we might each be responsible for our rose. Yet, a multitude of conditions and processes in the world act against this natural tendency toward relationship.

3.1 THE ROOTS OF ALIENATION

We take up the idea of relationality amidst the backdrop of modernity. What is the modern condition, and how does this affect the impulse to establish connections with one another? Without supposing that we can do justice to this expansive topic, it nevertheless would help our discussion to sketch some of the outlines of the modern perspective.

Ontologically speaking, we can partly trace the modern conception of the individual to the Cartesian notion of the rational being – *res cogitans* (or, the thinking thing). According to this perspective, the person is an autonomous ego regarding all things around it as a subject making judgments about the external world and the objects in it (including other beings). The Cartesian subject is a being wrapped up in individuality, pondering the external world like Rodin's Thinker or perhaps Hamlet perched high upon the castle ramparts, removed from the world, pondering one's existence.

The philosophy of the autonomous ego was reflected in ways of thinking, and corresponding social institutions, that reflected the radical separation of the individual from the other. One consequence was the emergence of the idea of the human person as a self-directed, utility maximizing machine.

Today, it would seem as if, the world over, life is dominated by the loss of relationality and an ever-present battle between self and the other. In tracing the growth of modern society, Weber describes the process of rationalization as objectification (Weber, 1920) where what might be nurturing relationships devolves into a means-end kind of functionalism. The other becomes less of a being like one's self and more of an object to be controlled. The worker becomes a nameless functionary in the assembly line of economic life (whether one works in sales, teaching, or in an actual factory). Rationalization is the reduction of the person's worth into whatever measure of productivity we impose – whether units of production in a plant or dollars of revenue. The reduction seems true whether in a completely liberalized society or a collectivized one. Being a student is rationalized into numbers on a standardized test – everywhere, from the SATs in the US to the *gaokao* in China. In a sense, persons themselves are rationalized, reduced to objects valued according to some functional yardstick.

Institutions are designed upon these means-ends relationships. However, this design comes at the expense of what should be rich, nurturing relationships between people, the other, and the earth. Horkheimer and Adorno (1972) likened the rationalization process to Ulysses tying himself to the mast of his ship in order to resist the siren song of nature. Marcuse (1964) describes the modern-day human as a one-dimensional being. In such a condition, the other becomes objectified, whose meaning to the self is reduced to the other's positive or negative valence (or reduced to nothing, as the other becomes invisible).

Of course, the world is not simply the rationalized wasteland the critical theorists described, but Weber's story is a powerful one, which we can interpret as a constant struggle between the relational being and the rationalized one. Rationalization is like a centrifugal impulse pushing people apart. It is less important for us to ascertain whether this splitting off of the rational from the relational was a process that occurred over a specific period in history, or was always at work in the human condition. At the heart of the conflict is the radical conceptualization of who or what the person is. Rationalization can take on different forms – whether, for functional purposes, the person is treated as a completely individualized being (in the liberal model) or a totally collectivized one (in a statist model). The person, as we will argue in the following pages, is a rich, complex being, something of, and more than, a dialectic between the individual and collective self. The human is not simply selfish and not simply selfless – so why would we model institutions upon such conceptualizations?

There were voices to the contrary, however. Several centuries after Descartes and the rationalists established the foundations of the modernist perspective, there arose other, non-Cartesian, perspectives on what it meant to be human. The phenomenologists, beginning with Husserl, claimed that the person was characterized by intentionality (or a tending toward an other). That is, we are not simply autonomous beings regarding all things around us from a distance. Rather, we are each beings that understand self and the world through relating with those around us. There is never just an individual mind but, instead, a person who is always tending or relating to another. The developmental psychologist, Jean Piaget, lent support to this notion by demonstrating how children, early in their development, form an understanding of who they are by relating to an other (beginning with their mother).

Such a reorientation from the autonomous individual to the connected self has ethical ramifications. Martin Buber described the relational in terms of a transition from an I-It perspective to I-Thou – that is, moving from the subject regarding an object to two subjects mutually acknowledging each other (Buber, 1937). Levinas suggested that encountering the other required not simply acknowledgment but a moral responsibility toward the other (Levinas, 1961). Carol Gilligan portrays the relationship with the other as constituting an ethical framework of care, within which all are part of a web of relationships. In this framework, reason, will, and feeling are relational, as opposed to the abstract, liberal ideal of the self. While an ethicist like Lawrence Kohlberg (1974) characterized moral development as the realization of abstract, universal principles, Gilligan described a different kind of moral reasoning which can be situated only in one's relationships with others. This conception of the person elucidates "the tie between relationship and responsibility, and the origins of aggression in the failure of connection" (Gilligan, 1993; see also Noddings, 2013).

While Gilligan did not describe care in ontological terms, she, nonetheless, taps into something that speaks to the nature of humankind, a movement from Descartes' *cogito ergo sum* (I think therefore I am) to something akin to *nos curare ergo sumus* (we care therefore we are).[1] Just as no one is simply an individual, in society, no one should be alone. In other words, we each have an innate responsibility to the other.

In this and subsequent chapters, we will understand relationality as also, necessarily, a reaction to the dimensions of alienation found in society, whether this be the dividing lines that are socially constructed between society and nature, the assumed divergence between the global "north" over "south," and privileging by gender, race, class, or other markers of difference. As an ethic, relationality can be seen as a countermovement to processes of differencing and exclusion.

The relationality of being, thought, and action finds support in different fields, including the experimental work described in the previous chapter. In the following sections, we take up several related fields of research.

3.2 THE PSYCHOLOGY OF RELATIONALITY

3.2.1 Egoism versus Altruism

Around the same time that Gilligan, Noddings, and others were exploring the philosophical and ethical foundations of relationality, researchers in the field of social psychology were producing evidence that suggested that other-regard was a basic dimension of the human psyche.

For some researchers, the central question was explaining seemingly altruistic behavior among humans, including the anomalies in the experimental games (like the ultimatum game) discussed earlier. Some asked whether altruism was really self-interest in disguise – for example, one can be generous to another in the hope or expectation of receiving similar generosity in the future (recall the tit-for-tat strategy). Or perhaps giving is really a way to enhance one's social reputation. Perhaps it is mostly a way of conforming to social norms found in one's group. Each of these,

---

[1] Tronto (2017) refers to the human being as *homines curans*.

and other hypotheses, are alternatives to the purely altruistic motivation which is that a person might give to another solely or mostly for the good of the other. Before we discuss the experimental evidence, note that all of these psychological explanations could potentially be valid, some more valid in some situations than others. There is evidence in support of each of these mechanisms in differing contexts. We will discuss the research that suggests that, in situations such as the experimental games we discussed, some (or many) people do indeed give mainly because they want to help the other.

The fact is that humans often behave altruistically. The systematic anomalies found in the experimental game literature suffice to show that people give more than economic theory predicts they should (e.g., Dawes & Thaler, 1988; Camerer & Thaler, 1995; Bolton & Ockenfels, 2000).

The question is: why? In one lab experiment, Batson and Moran (1999) had college students participate in a version of the prisoner's dilemma game. Before playing the game, the participants were asked to read a note from the other (anonymous) player describing a personal ordeal. Half of participants were given instructions to try and imagine what the other person was going through, and the other half were asked to try and be objective despite reading the note. They confirmed their hypothesis that the group asked to take the perspective of the other would act more cooperatively in the game. Batson and colleagues reasoned that altruism was triggered by empathy, which they defined as "a set of congruent vicarious emotions, those that are more other-focused than self-focused, including feelings of sympathy, compassion, tenderness, and the like" (Batson & Shaw, 1991, 113). In their theory, empathy had two essential elements: first, recognizing the "other" as a being of value and, second, recognizing need in the other.

The question is whether charitable behavior is due to altruism or a disguised kind of egoism, a question raised as early as the writings of Comte (1851). When a person gives to a charity, for example, is it really out of concern for the welfare for the recipient (altruism), or is it something that ultimately is done for the benefit of the giver (egoism). As an example of the egoistic pathway, does giving reduce the discomfort one is feeling over the suffering of another, increase one's feeling of satisfaction or self-esteem or goodness, or increase the likelihood that the giver receive reciprocal benefits in kind in the future? Models of these types of egoism can be found in Cialdini et al.'s negative state relief theory (Cialdini et al., 1973a), or Andreoni's warm glow hypothesis (Andreoni, 1990). One can categorize the reciprocity dimension in the repeated game as belonging to the egoism hypothesis.

Though the debate is far from settled, a considerable store of evidence has accumulated in support of the altruism hypothesis. For example, Batson and colleagues designed studies to test whether a person's willingness to help a subject being subjected to painful stimulus was due to the helping person's need to reduce their own feelings of discomfort or due to their empathizing with the subject. The result was a dominance of the empathy motivation, to the point that some participants would volunteer to take on the painful stimulus themselves to relieve the subject in distress (Batson, 1987). Other researchers have obtained comparable results showing that prosocial behavior was linked to empathy inducement and not to the need to escape personal discomfort (e.g., Lee & Murningham, 2001; Stocks, Lishner, & Decker, 2009).

Another possibility is that the participant helps to avoid any possible negative social evaluation (e.g., from the researcher). However, Fultz et al., (1986) found that willingness to help did not vary whether the participants were told that others would know about their actions or that no one could possibly know. These results support a kind of altruism that takes effect apart from considerations of reputation, reciprocity, or social sanction. To take another example, Rumble, Van Lange, and Parks (2010) had subjects play a prisoner's dilemma type game, in which opponents deviated occasionally from the cooperative strategy. They found that players with high empathic concern were more willing to forgive these deviations and act benevolently, contrary to a predominantly reciprocal or normative response.

Yet other researchers suggest that people may be motivated more by a moral commitment to care than by empathy (e.g., Wilhelm & Bekkers, 2010). But these different motivational reasons need not be mutually exclusive. People may well experience multiple motivations simultaneously, and which pathways to altruism dominate maybe situation-dependent. While the work of Batson et al., supports the role of empathic concern in fostering altruism, we should recognize that multiple motivations may often act in concert to move people to charitable behavior. As Sen (2009) put it, people have a "plurality of reasons" for their actions. In this book, our relational perspective on collective action is eclectic in this regard, not requiring that one tease out which particular route leads from connectedness to prosocial behavior, so long as some pathway(s) are activated. Connectedness, in the form of some kind of cognizance of or contact with a particular other, can be an important factor, whatever the prevailing motivational mechanism. That is, one may need to recognize a tangible other in order to trigger empathic concern or perspective taking. Similarly, some egoism-related pathways, such as reducing suffering of the other in order to reduce one's own discomfort, may also require connectedness in order for the subject to know of the other's condition.

Empathy, moreover, is a general concept that encompasses a range of relevant meanings. On the one hand, we use the term, empathy, for a kind of affinitive feeling, where the other's joy or sorrow leads to an experience of joy and sorrow in ourselves, as well. But it can also pertain to a mode of perception. As Edith Stein was careful to point out, the other's experience is something that is not experienced by us firsthand (or primordially) but, rather, we can perceive the experience in the other and, by extension, recognize the other as an experiencing being (Stein, 1964).

3.2.2 Social/Psychological Distance

Psychological distance (or proximity) is a concept encompassing a broad class of conditions that loosely represent varying types and degrees of connectedness (or disconnectedness). Wang et al., (2019) define psychological distance as "a theoretical construct that refers to the subjective perception of distance between the self and some object or event" (Wang et al., 2019, 2). Clearly, there are multiple dimensions to psychological distance – for example, some researchers break it down into four categories: spatial, temporal, social, and theoretical corresponding to "when [an event] occurs, where it occurs, to whom it occurs and whether it occurs" (Trope & Liberman, 2010, 442). The hypothesis is that, when psychological distance increases (or decreases), one's tendency to care about something decreases (or increases).

A growing body of evidence suggests that, at least in some situations, some dimensions of psychological distance affect people's concern about a social or environmental problem and their willingness to act on it (Maiella et al., 2020a). For example, Chu and Yang (2018) found that portraying climate change with proximate/familiar cues, as compared to distant/unfamiliar ones, reduced polarization around the issue. There seems to be more studies that focus on the spatial dimension of psychological distance. Some studies have shown a greater concern for an issue like climate when it is described in localized terms (e.g., Spence & Pidgeon, 2010; Scanell & Gifford, 2011; Jones, Hine, & Marks, 2017). Some other studies have not found localization to be as significant (e.g., Schuldt, Rickard, & Yang, 2018; Brügger, 2020).

But less attention seems to have been paid to the effect of varying the social dimension of distance.

It is the social dimension of psychological distance that is most relevant to our discussion. In some cases, the social dimension can be the most relevant of the different aspects of psychological distance – for example, Spence et al., (2012) found the social dimension to be most associated with preparedness to act on climate change. It has been noted, for example, that empathic concern may give way to obligation in the case of helping family and other close relations, and be stronger with respect to groups a little more socially removed (Davis, 2015). This leads us to considerations of social and psychological distance and their effect on empathy.

One straightforward manifestation of social and psychological distance is seen in different reactions people have vis-a-vis an identified versus unidentified recipient of aid. Considerable research suggests that identifiable recipients of aid motivate more giving as compared to anonymous recipients (Small & Loewenstein, 2003). Kogut and Ritov (2005) found that pledged contributions for a needy child were significantly higher when the name and photograph of the child was provided. This reflects our earlier point, that connectedness transforms anonymous to particular others.[2] Recall the results of the dictator game described in Chapter 2. Many people are moved to give to a cause, but giving can take on a special meaning when it is for a particular recipient.

Another type of social distance or proximity has to do with whether the "other" is a member of one's in-group or part of an out-group. Tajfel and colleagues, early on, conducted research suggesting that people will exhibit favoritism for people in their in-group, even when these classifications are arbitrary and no real conflicts of interest exist between groups (Tajfel et al., 1971). Researchers have explored the connection between group affiliation and prosocial behavior (e.g., see Aksoy & Palma, 2019). Some have explored the opposite effect, where manipulating the experimental situation such that the participant is made to feel some type of exclusion was seen to lead to less empathic concern and less altruistic behavior (e.g., see DeWall & Baumeister, 2006; Twenge et al., 2007). This helps us understand the role of social networks in

---

[2] The effect of identifiability may not hold as much, however, when the "other" is an already known person – for example, McClough et al., (2015) found that showing photographs of students receiving aid, to potential donors from the same school, resulted in smaller donations. In this case, social distance does not seem to govern.

fostering collective action – we simply generalize the idea of in-group with that of the social network.

Individual traits can influence psychological distance. In a series of investigations, Batson et al., studied whether similarity in individual traits (e.g., attitudes and interests) influenced helping behavior. They concluded that such behavior did increase in the case of an other who was more similar to the decision-maker (Batson et al., 1979, 1981). Similarly, Aron et al., (1992) propose that very close ties (e.g., family, spouse) lead to inclusion of others in the perception of self. This dynamic allows us to understand significant acts of altruism that span across generations.

This does not mean that altruism is reserved only for others in one's immediate social network (or, more broadly, those exhibiting social homophily). Graziano et al., (2007) found that perspective taking can lead to greater altruism toward members of the out-group, as well (in this case, one takes the perspective of the out-group member). Our theory should be flexible about the degree of specificity of the "other," being open to degrees of variation in the spectrum between the generalized and particular other (Benhabib, 1987).

What about extraordinary generosity displayed toward even more distant others? Empathic concern has dimensions that are also affective in nature, which might predispose a person toward altruistic sentiments toward many and not just the person's immediate social or kin group. Barraza and Zak (2009) experimented with an ultimatum game in which participants viewed a video, beforehand, that was either sad (thus presumably evoking empathic concern) or not, showing that participants viewing the sad video exhibited greater generosity. Interestingly, the subject of the video was not in any way related to the recipient of the game's payoff, which suggests that when empathy has an affective dimension, it tends to extend in a general way to others. There is literature suggesting that people's empathy is "malleable" and that people find ways to develop greater empathy for dissimilar others (Schumann, Zaki, & Dweck, 2014). Johnston and Glasford (2018) conduct research showing how increasing the quantity (and, more importantly to the researchers, quality) of interpersonal contact with people from an outgroup increased empathy and a helping attitude for the outgroup members. There is support, from research on neurobiology, that also supports the idea that the human capacity for empathy is broad and extends to dissimilar others (e.g., Lamm, Meltzoff, & Decety, 2010). Majdandžić et al., (2016) showed how mentalizing (or perspective-taking) with a dissimilar other increased prosocial attitudes toward them. In the next section, we describe some neurobiological evidence in support of relationality.

In the last chapter of the book, we take up the specific example of climate change and revisit the idea of social and psychological distance in the context of climate action.

3.3 NEUROBIOLOGICAL DIMENSIONS OF RELATIONALITY

Another emerging field of study focuses on the neurobiological effects or antecedents of altruistic behavior. In some cases, researchers have combined neurobiological measurements with simulated experimental economic games (such as the ultimatum game) described earlier.

A simple notion of empathy is the ability or tendency of a person to feel what the other feels, sometimes referred to as emotional empathy. It has been known for some time now that witnessing someone experiencing pain or distress activates the same higher brain areas (e.g., the anterior to the mid cingulate cortex) as when one experiences pain or distress oneself (Preston and de Waal, 2002). Similarly, Preis et al. (2015) use fMRI data to show that perceiving pain in another activates similar neurological pathways as one's own perception of pain. Conversely, one's own experience of pain is seen to increase empathy for others (Eklund et al., 2009). Emotional empathy operates in humans even in early infancy and is associated with increased activity in the anterior cingulate and insula (Shamy-Tsoory et al., 2009). Such phenomena need not register automatically with the subject and can be modulated by one's interpretation of the other's experience (Singer et al., 2006). These studies suggest that perhaps humans are "hard-wired" for empathic concern.

In some literature, a distinction is made between affective empathy, where one experiences what the other experiences, and cognitive empathy, where one is able to take the perspective of the other (e.g., Smith, 2006). Affective and cognitive empathy may involve interacting areas of the brain. The anterior insular and anterior cingulate cortices have been shown to be activated during the empathic witnessing of another's pain (e.g., Gu et al., 2012), which is a central aspect of affective empathy. Studying fMRI data of participants watching video of a person expressing pain following a medical procedure, Lamm et al., (2007) found that the viewing of pain shared neural pathways with the firsthand experience of it.

On the part of cognitive empathy, some studies suggest that reflection on one's self as well as the subjective perspective of others activates the inferior parietal complex (e.g., Johnson et al., 2002; Decety & Grèzes, 2006). There is evidence, furthermore, that this phenomenon can be enhanced by perspective taking, often referred to as cognitive empathy (drawing a distinction between this and emotional empathy). In some investigations, cognitive empathy, involving perspective-taking, seemed to activate areas of the brain, such as the tempoparietal junction, different from that seen with emotional empathy.[3]

Thus, there is a possibility that neural pathways for emotional empathy might be triggered more strongly when the person experiencing the condition is close to the subject, while empathy for more distant others, requiring mentalizing the other's emotion, activates pathways associated with cognitive empathy (Majdandžić et al., 2016).

There is evidence for other pathways to altruism, some perhaps compatible with egoistic theories of altruism. For example, compassionate actions activate the brain's reward system, resulting in the release of dopamine as a "reward" for the altruistic behavior. This also can reduce the experience of pain during empathy (Klimecki et al., 2014). Harbaugh, Mayr, and Burghart (2007) found an increased level of activation of striatal regions of the brain when individuals donate to a charity versus keeping money for themselves, supporting a warm-glow motivation of altruism.

The literature on the neurobiology of empathy distinguishes between cognitive and affective modes of empathy, the assumption being that different neural pathways are responsible for each (McCreary et al., 2018). Cognitive empathy tends to be associated with perspective taking (e.g., Carré et al., 2013), while affective empathy involves sharing the other's emotions (e.g., de Waal, 2008). There is some evidence that affective empathy develops earlier in a person's development than cognitive empathy, the affective route being involuntary and involving somato-sensorimotor resonance, even mimicry, between self and other (Decety, 2011).

Empathic concern can also be increased through social learning. In experiments involving a prisoner's dilemma game, Rilling et al., (2012) show that participants involved in reciprocated cooperation experience reward through oxytocin and dopamine learning pathways that show

---

[3] Note that some scholars carefully delineate between empathy and perspective taking – for example, Galinsky et al., (2008) associate perspective taking with a cognitive ability to consider the world from other viewpoints, while they define empathy as an affection connection with another. Furthermore, in their research on negotiation, these authors found that perspective taking was more conducive to better outcomes than empathy.

increased activity over time. Zak and Barazza develop a model in which empathic concern and altruistic collection action are primed by increases in oxytocin. In a version of the ultimatum game, they showed that intra-nasal doses of oxytocin resulted in an 80 percent increase in generosity of the giver compared to the placebo group (Barazza & Zak, 2013). Previous research has implicated oxytocin in empathic concern – for example, Domes et al., (2007) showed that oxytocin infusion enhances one's ability to infer emotion and intention from gazing at another's facial expression. Oxytocin may increase the salience of social cues (e.g., facial expression) and help the subject focus more closely on them (Perez-Rodriguez, 2015). In one experiment, Zak et al., (2007) showed that receiving a gift or pay-ment increased oxytocin in the recipients, prompting them to be more generous in return, a finding that supports a reciprocity pathway to altru-ism. Further work, however, also supported altruism not directly linked to reciprocity – for example, viewing an emotional video primed higher levels of oxytocin, followed by increased generosity to a recipient not related to the video (Barraza & Zak, 2009). We might conjecture that these endocrine mechanisms maybe found in multiple pathways to other-regard (e.g., warm-glow effects versus empathy), making it more difficult to neatly distinguish them. In the end, we have to be open to a number of consonant mechanisms, and empathic concern maybe both learned and innate (e.g., see Ridley, 2003).

3.4 EVOLUTIONARY CONSIDERATIONS

If at least part of the other-regarding tendencies of people are due to innate mechanisms, then the question arises as to why this came about in the evolution of the species. Why competitive advantage might have existed for behavior that often comes at a price to the giving individual?

The logic is not difficult in the case of one's kin. Self-sacrifice for one's family is almost a universal feature of human societies, in some cases, extreme self-sacrifice. Parenting is the classic model of caring for the other. As much as many, perhaps most, children resolve to "give back" to their parents later on in their lives, the fact is that much of this is a debt that goes unpaid. Nonetheless, it is not hard to work out an evolution-ary logic for parenting. As some point out, such altruistic behavior helps to maintain the genetic lineage, conferring an evolutionary advantage to those clans where parents exert great efforts to protect and nurture their progeny (e.g., Krupp et al., 2008; Stewart-Williams, 2007). This behav-ior is common among other species, as well (Alcock, 1993).

But what about extreme generosity toward the nonfamilial other, even the stranger? What possible explanation might one offer, in evolutionary terms? The hypotheses offered by the literature span various shades of egoism and even to the altruistic. One evolutionary explanation is based on the logic of the repeated game – that is, the type of reciprocity reflected in a strategy like tit-for-tat. The logic requires that people (or their genes) take a longer view of fitness and survival (Harris & Madden, 2002). Generosity maybe costly for the person in the short-run, but it may redound back to the individual over time (Barclay, 2012). Such altruism fits the reciprocity hypothesis when generous acts favor others in a person's community, provided the community is maintained over time to the benefit of the giver. This is Ostrom's thesis, in fact. Heritable adaptations on the level of the group can include tendencies to monitor and sanction, rule-setting, and other properties of communal systems (Wilson et al., 2008). But the advantage is less obvious when altruism is directed at the non-proximate other who conceivably never have a chance to reciprocate.

There are several ways of arguing through the issue of generosity toward the non-reciprocating stranger. The first is to recognize, that "natural selection is a very blunt instrument" (Barclay & Van Vugt, 2015, 19). Altruism toward the stranger maybe a by-product of other evolutionary products. For example, benevolence toward others in one's community may have resulted in traits that "bleed over" onto relationships with the general other. Another possibility is that empathy maybe a by-product of another evolutionary development such as selection for abilities to learn from others. For example, the ability to imitate behavior in others might be influenced by so-called "mirror neurons." These same mirror neurons are suspected to also factor in one's ability to form internal representations of others' actions and motives – in other words, to empathize (Keysers & Gazzola, 2006).

Yet another possibility is through a kind of "cultural selection," where groups with strong prosocial orientations attract members more strongly than other groups. Furthermore, as the argument goes, since prosocial behavior endows advantages to the group, then more prosocial groups replace less prosocial groups. Similarly, these prosocial cultural norms can displace other norms (Boyd & Richerson, 2002).

Beyond all these considerations, we should be open even to possibilities that human behavior and culture develop in ways that cannot be explained in ways consistent with evolutionary pressure. The person, and the group, maybe infinitely more complex than the gene or the species.

Systems of thought may exist and endure in a manner independent of evolutionary forces. The Teduray, a forest-dwelling community in the Philippines, have an overriding social norm that revolves around "preserving the other's gall bladder," a norm that generalizes to simply caring for the other. When shown a film of people playing baseball, members of the Teduray tribe expressed confusion about the nature of a game, asking why one would want to score more points than the other (Schlegel, 2003). Human behavior can display a motivational autonomy such that "its motivation becomes disconnected from its ultimate goals... humans have the ability to care not only for their offspring but also for out-group members and even animals of other species" (Decety, 2011, 8).

3.5 CONCLUDING THOUGHTS

As the wealth of evidence from the sciences suggests, empathy and other-regard are essential parts of the human condition. It is therefore strange to realize that many models of human behavior, political economy, and institutions mostly neglect it. Decision theory is founded mainly on a rational choice framework that emphasizes the maximization of individual utility. Few scholars of rational choice would say that humans think and behave only according to individual utility maximization, but their models of human behavior essentially do this. Now consider: what if the models were more faithful to the ways that people think and behave? How would this affect how we design institutions?

Our proposal is simply to re-orient our ideas and models about human behavior and the institutions modeled upon them to reflect other-regard. As Batson and Shaw (1991, 120) suggest: "The evidence supporting the empathy-altruism hypothesis suggests the presence of a valuable untapped natural resource in our efforts to build a more caring, humane society."

In the next chapter, we examine some of the ways that empathy and other-regard work to foster collective action and prosocial behavior in a wide range of circumstances. We will be more liberal, at least more so than the literature reviewed in this chapter, about how exactly different people define empathy. For example, while the previous literature was careful to distinguish between cognitive and affective empathy, throughout the rest of this book, we will treat these as if they occurred together (which they often do).

4

Connectedness and Pro-Social/Pro-Environmental Behavior

In Chapter 3, we reviewed some of the evidence regarding just how complex we humans are. Part of that complexity is derived from how much our identities are wrapped up in our relationships with others. Relationality is what makes us most deeply human, and enabling people to connect with each other is a turn towards living fully authentic lives.

We now examine how connectedness and ensuing empathy can foster particular types of collective action. In the following chapter, we will look at situations that closely resemble what Ostrom and colleagues investigated when they studied common problems. All of the examples we discuss in this chapter also belong to what is correctly understood as the commons. Hunger and loss of livelihood from environmental degradation and desertification are problems of the commons – that is, nobody "owns" these problems, and responding to them face classic barriers to collective action such as free ridership. Likewise, the ongoing threat to endangered species and their habitat is a common issue, as is, we will argue, the general problem of disregarding nonhuman beings. In all of these cases, a part of the problem lies in the distance between these issues and people's everyday concerns. The question is the same: in these situations, what does it take to reduce our alienation from the other? In other words, what does it take for people to care?

4.1 MORE ON THE ROOTS OF ALIENATION

In Chapter 3, we considered the idea that modernist thinking has been at least partially behind the alienation that people experience today. However, another aspect of this alienation may have to do with how we have materially arranged our lifestyles and, in particular, structured the cities around which our lives revolve.

Modern-day life, especially for residents of the busy metropolis, is fraught with disconnect. Part of this is a social condition, in which people in the city can find themselves strewn about like flotsam and jetsam in a sea of strangers. Durkheim (1893) attributes this to the replacement of connections between self and others in the community or small town (which he strangely referred to as mechanical solidarity) by the more functionalist and impersonal connections in the metropolis (which he strangely referred to as organic solidarity). Wirth (1938) refers to the feeling of living amidst a faceless, placeless city as anomie.

The alienation is material, as well, and it is most evident in our relationships with the natural world. Today, one can go to a large supermarket (or its online outlet) and buy coffee from thousands of miles away. Most urbanites have no inkling of where their goods come from, in what manner they are produced, and by whom. There is a concept of a foodshed – that is, the land where one's food is sourced. The problem with applying the concept is that the modern-day foodshed, for most people who have the means to live a modern consumer lifestyle, is almost unbounded. We would not begin to be able to trace where we source our food. Cities have long disattached themselves from their hinterland (Billen, Ganier, & Barles, 2012). A cheese sandwich might have had its origins in wheat from a farm in Durham, North Carolina, cheese from a dairy in Salerno, and paprika from Hyderabad – but most importantly, the consumer wouldn't have a clue. All we see is the thing on our plate.

In short, we have all been disconnected (to varying degrees) from the natural world. In the pre-modern way of life, which we still see in the vestiges of hunter-gatherer communities around the world, there was no choice but to have an intimate relationship with the natural world. This connection shows up in their knowledge of the natural world – consider the many distinctions (and terms) used by the Teduray for palm trees, or the Inuit for types of snow.

Some of this natural connection was severed with the arrival of the more modern, more sedentary, way of life afforded by agriculture (said to have begun in the fertile crescent in the Middle East). Agriculture made possible the dawning of the early city (Mumford, 1961). In the city, one need not be a primary producer, since farmers lived on the outskirts of the ancient city, and city residents were free to engage in other pursuits (e.g., masonry, weaving, teaching). Nevertheless, these early consumers still had some sense of connection. They would know where their wheat came

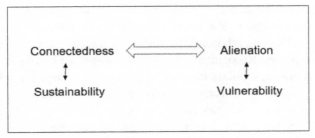

FIGURE 4.1 The dialectic of connectedness and alienation.

from, how it came to them, and by whose hands it came – the early city's foodshed was limited to a small radius encircling the city (a radius limited by the ability of early producers to transport their produce to the city with wheeled carts before they spoiled).

However, the industrial age, beginning in the latter part of the nineteenth century, severed this natural connection between primary and secondary consumption. Today, foodstuffs, clothing, and almost every other necessity of urban life can be shipped or flown in from any part of the globalized world. In such a world, the connection with the other becomes invisible – first with the human other, but as importantly, with the rest of the natural world. Part of the problem has to do with knowledge: we no longer know who the other is, what the other is experiencing. It also has to do with disempathy: when the other is invisible to us, then we do not (or cannot) care for the other.

Hunger, species extinction, habitat loss, climate change – these are among the most pressing issues that can seem distant to many in the urbanized world. So, the question becomes: how do we reestablish our connections with these issues, which means, how do we restore our connection to the distant other?

Part of the solution must come from accessing the part of ourselves that tends toward relationship and connection, rather than just isolation and self-regard. If care is an essential part of the human condition, then it manifests itself whenever people are given the chance to connect with each other. This is an important point: *when obstacles (whether physical, social, or institutional) to interconnection are removed, and where routes to encountering the other are available, people's natural tendency to relate to the other can be activated.*

The concept opposite to that of alienation is relationship and connectedness (see Figure 4.1). In promoting relationships, we seek to undo the divide

between the subject and the other, and the way that the other is objectified into lesser things that serve merely to advance the ego's interest. We
seek active, affirming relationships with the other, whether other people,
animals, or places. Recognizing that relationships can be forged between
people and places, scholars have coined the term, topophilia, which was
coined to capture the affective/cognitive/moral tie between a person and
place, and the way such ties enrich one's life (Tuan, 1990; Ogunseitan,
2005). Others have turned to the concept of assemblage (a term from
Deleuze & Guattari, 1987), or more-than-human conceptualizations of
social-ecological systems, as ways to reverse the strong polarity between
self and other (e.g., Spies & Alff, 2020). In this literature, an assemblage
is simply a socio-spatial formation made up of heterogeneous elements,
including human and nonhuman (Anderson & McFarlane, 2011). But
what is the coming together of elements if not entering into relationship?
The relational view sees the other as no longer passive and inert but as pos-
sessing moral worth and agency (Schmidt & Dowsley, 2010).

In the following sections, we consider evidence of relationality at work
in everyday examples of pro-social and pro-environmental behavior.

4.2 RELATIONALITY AND CHARITABLE DONATIONS

In a field study, researchers set up posters requesting donations to end
world hunger in convenience stores around a neighborhood (Thornton,
Kirchner, & Jacobs, 1991). In half of the sites, the posters contained just
the text of the appeal, while in the other half, the posters showed a photograph of a child with a tear on his cheek. They found that, on average,
donations at the sites with the photograph-bearing posters were almost
double that in the no-photograph condition. In another study, Genevsky
et al. (2013) found that participants in a donation experiment were more
than twice as likely to donate (actual money) when the appeal showed the
photograph of the child/recipient compared to showing only a silhouette
(see also Zarzycka, 2016).

As discussed in Chapter 3, considerable research supports the idea
that reducing "psychological distance" helps foster altruism by triggering
empathy. Giving can result from emotional empathy, which is an almost
automatic sensorimotor response to someone suffering. It can also occur
through cognitive empathy, which involves some sort of perspective-taking
by the donor of someone in need. In either case, what is required is to
draw attention to the *particular*, instead of the abstract, other. The other
requirement is that the donor recognize that the potential recipient is in

need (Schwartz, 1970; Batson et al., 2002) and deserving of help (Miller, 1977; Furnham, 1995). And yet, at the same time, the care triggered by connection with a particular other extends, in many cases, to the *general* other as well. Note that people give in these cases even when their donation is not routed directly to the child or adult shown in the photograph but to an organization that works in this area (and, presumably, to the general community to which the child or adult belongs). Perhaps the discrepancy between the "small-N" solution and the "large-N" problem is not as problematic in reality as they might appear to be in the rarified air of the mathematical model (presented in Chapter 2).

Clearly, the identifiability of the recipient of aid can lead to emotional empathy (Kogut & Ritov, 2011). Charities have known this for years. Many charitable organizations purposely show photographs of recipients, as they intuitively identify this to be an effective fundraising strategy (Burt & Strongman, 2005; Hibbert et al., 2007; O'Dell, 2008; Small & Verroci, 2009).

Reducing psychological distance, however, can be done even without the use of photographs. Small and Loewenstein (2003) showed that even just informing the donor that a recipient family has already been chosen can result in an increase in donations. The most direct connection allows the donor to sponsor a specific individual, which many organizations choose to do (Zagefka & James, 2015).

4.3 RELATIONALITY AND ENVIRONMENTAL CONSERVATION

These results imply that our pro-social selves make themselves known when the "other" is not an abstraction but a particular someone. Furthermore, this beneficence can diffuse out from the particular other to many others. Recall the experimental game described in Chapter 2, where showing potential donors a picture of children playing around trees in a forest leads to an increase in donations for reforestation. Researchers have also found empathy for the nonhuman other to be a primary reason behind pro-environmental behavior, such as donating towards species conservation (e.g., Berenguer, 2007).

As noted, empathy is most easily triggered when encountering the specific, individual other but also extends to a general magnanimity. Altruism and generosity can "spill over" onto other parties beyond the particular other in question. Recall, from Chapter 3, how activating empathy for one suffering other leads to an increased donation to a different individual in the experimental game. Similarly, although it may be true that "fellow-feeling" might be assumed most likely when the other is just like us (Miller et al., 2019; Wei & Liu, 2020), much evidence also tells us that empathy can extend to dissimilar others (Majdandžić et al., 2016). We can only speculate why this is so. Perhaps those qualities that make us imagine another as not so different from ourselves that we can imagine their predicament, have less to do with traits we assume to define similarity (e.g., race, nationality, etc.), and perhaps more to do with our commonality on the plane of experiencing (joy, suffering, excitement, etc.). Or perhaps it is the combination of affective and cognitive empathy, and their expansive reach, that allows us this flexibility. These are open questions. For our needs, it suffices to understand that there is a certain inductive quality to empathy, where it can start with a concern for the particular other and end with an openness and regard for the general other, as well.

In the previous sections, we discussed how relationality involves, in many cases, seeing the particular other. This should hold true in the case of nonhuman others, as well. Consider how the little prince began to understand how his fox was not just one of a million other foxes, and his rose not just one of a million other roses. Animals or not simply a genus or species – rather, they are particular others and to be valued as such. It should not be such a radical concept to realize that the nonhuman other is a valued being. After all, this is what it means for a child to form a relationship with a pet. Perhaps the earth's salvation lies in the idea that every child should have a pet (or every pet should have a child).

Connecting with the other can be transformative. The experience of caring for a pet can make for a more caring human with regard to the more general, nonhuman other. Researchers have found that pet ownership correlates with increased valuing of animals and a lowered approval of hunting (e.g., Prokop & Tunnicliffe, 2010; Binngiesser et al., 2013). Paul and Serpell (1996) found that caring for a pet as a child correlated with later support for and membership in environmental organizations as an adult (also see Bennett, 2003). Other types of species encounter, early in life, can lead to pro-environmental values later on as well (Preston et al., 2021). Caring for the other nurtures the relational part of our selves.

It is not surprising, then, that human empathy can extend to nonhuman others (specially to animate beings such as our pets, mammals in the wild, and others). People who feel more compassion for other humans tend to also do so for nonhuman species as well (Pfattheicher, Sassenrath, & Schindler, 2016). Just as seeing a picture of another human in need can foster giving, some researchers have found a similar effect with regard to animals. Some researchers have found the identifiable victim effect to pertain also to animals, most markedly among people who do not profess strong environmentalism (Markowitz et al., 2013).

The picture need not even be real. Whitley, Kalof, and Flach (2020) found that portraits of animals (photographed in studio settings) elicit even greater empathy than photographs in natural settings. In another experiment, researchers found that emotional attachment to a virtual polar bear was connected to increased commitment toward environmentally friendly actions (Dillahunt et al., 2008).

Some researchers have found that perspective taking can extend to other species (Schultz, 2000; Sevillano, Aragonés, & Schultz, 2007). "Conversely, nurturance has been suggested to influence empathy, in that humans have an ability to empathise with non-kin in a similar way as with their own offspring when certain characteristics (e.g., childlikeness) are present," write Prguda and Neumann (2014), suggesting that more generalized empathy for the other has its roots in the bond between mother and infant. We can even imagine the experience of non-animate living things.[1] While contact with one species can lead to a general empathy with other species (e.g., Amiot & Bastian, 2015), the human capacity to care is not unbounded, and biases occur. For example, some researchers point to morphological similarity or "cuddliness" (Smith et al., 2012) as a basis for how much empathy feel towards different species (e.g., Figure 4.2). One can expect people to donate more towards pandas than tarantulas. Miralles, Raymond, and Lecointre (2019) suggest that affinity decreases with evolutionary divergence in time.

When physical similarity is not enough, there is the possibility of representing nonhumans in humanlike ways. Though aware of possible dangers of anthropomorphizing, some conservationists nevertheless recognize the role of anthropomorphism in increasing the public's empathy for, and willingness to protect, nonhuman species (e.g., Chan, 2012; Young, Khalil, & Wharton, 2018).

---

[1] In one elementary school class in Hong Kong, the author observed the teachers encourage the students to sit on the beach and imagine themselves to be a mangrove tree in the intertidal zone. Later, Dean Johnson, teacher, takes the students kayaking and stops just short of the beach. The reason, he said, is not only do students have fun jumping into the water and splashing around, but it is important for these young environmentalists to encounter their environment in the most direct ways possible. In another meeting, local ecologist, Nicola Newbery, creates an exercise where students look for mangrove propagules on the beach and replant them in a good location. Taking perspective-taking a step further, in one class, the students play a game where students take assigned roles (including a lobster, mud skipper, and others) and act out these parts. The kids seemed to have a good time, especially the lobsters.

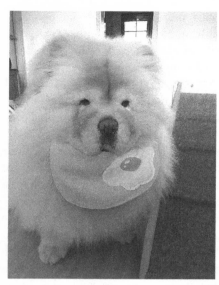

FIGURE 4.2 Cute animals foster emotional attachment. (Source: R. Lejano).

In one field experiment, farmers given a message encouraging them to take the perspective of others (including wildlife) affected by soil and water degradation were more likely to sign up for a state program supporting conservation efforts (Czap et al., 2015). Beneficiaries need not be human – Batavia et al. (2018) showed that providing survey respondents messages supporting empathy for wildlife were as or more effective than messages pertaining only to humans in soliciting donations for a conservation organization. The point is that, people show greater support for ecological conservation when they can perceive or see who benefits from conservation (whether people, animals, or trees).

Conservation groups have used our capacity for identifying with the other to great advantage, but the potential for even greater impacts from relationality seems still relatively untapped. We only need to think of the innumerable things we do in our daily round that damage the environment and contribute to the loss of habitat and species. People can be attuned to nature right in their very backyard, learning to see and hear the nonhuman other. Maybe all that is needed are different ways that such nature can be foregrounded, using strategies for pointing out to people the life around them (Čapek, 2010).

4.4 RELATIONALITY AND SUSTAINABLE, FAIR-TRADE CONSUMERISM

There has been a turn toward strategies aimed at incentivizing sustainable consumerism, including initiatives around pricing carbon, ecosystem services, and recycling. These efficiency-based strategies rely on egoist decision-making, which we acknowledge as a valid route toward sustainability. However, we underscore the need to, at the same time, build on the potential for altruistic attitudes and behavior on the part of the public (e.g., Bolderdijk et al., 2013; Dietz, 2015). Studies of consumer "types" agree that both egoistic and altruistic attitudes abound among the public (e.g., Sojka, 1986; Hirsch & Dolderman, 2007).

When people care, they go beyond the price of the good. In other words, consumption becomes something more than maximizing consumer surplus. Fair trade coffee, if truly practiced and certified, will not be priced lower than some other brands of coffee and can be significantly more expensive (Naegele, 2020). Yet, the demand for fair trade coffee is, in fact, increasing year by year. Researchers note how many people are willing to pay a significant extra premium to get coffee that is certified fair trade – as much as $3 extra per pound (Naegele, 2020). In one survey of fair trade coffee buyers, foremost among the reasons given for such a purchase have to do with alleviating suffering and poor working conditions among farm workers and their families (Darian et al., 2015).

Relationality adds an important dimension to strategies like eco-labeling and information-based regulation. While it is true that a primary reason for these policy instruments is to give the public more information about consumer products and businesses, another is that these devices can be used to connect "the x and the y" by providing people with some route to seeing and knowing about the particular other.

4.5 RELATIONALITY AND ENVIRONMENTAL JUSTICE

In the early hours of December 3, 1984, the Union Carbide pesticide plant in Bhopal, India, began leaking lethal methyl isocyanate gas from one of its tanks. The tank began to fail and, within two hours, about forty tons of the gas had escaped and engulfed the nearby towns, suffocating residents as they slept. Some estimate that about 8,000 people were killed in the immediate aftermath, and more than 100,000 injured (Eckerman, 2005). Investigations later revealed the extent of the negligence involved in the construction, maintenance, and operation of the plant (Sarangi, 2002). In the succeeding legal battle, Union Carbide eventually agreed to compensate the victims and their families, paying an average of 100,000 rupees (approximately USD 1,200) per fatality (Kumar, 2004). Though charged in court, the CEO for Union Carbide never appeared to face the charges.

We ask, how is it that some communities are essentially demarcated as sacrifice zones, subject to industrial, environmental, and other blight? How is it possible for a court to equate someone's life with some nominal monetary sum (and, moreover, assign a sum equal to that of a shoulder bag from some fashion district)?

Relationality cuts both ways. Just as connectedness can (at least in some cases) foster collective action, disconnectedness plays a part in the alienation and maltreatment of the other. The literature on environmental justice has, for some decades now, built up evidence of the systematic exposure of some communities to cumulative burdens from poor air and water, crumbling infrastructure, lack of amenities, and other issues. In many places, the neighborhoods that find themselves with these multiple burdens are lower-income, often with a high proportion of ethnic minorities, often places where languages are spoken that sound foreign to the majority.[2]

The inherent inequity in global climate negotiations is another example of this, as nations who have contributed far less to the climate problem than developed nations suffer disproportionately from its effects – it is essentially a global commons (Agarwal et al., 2017). This and other environmental justice issues can be thought of as collective action problems as well. The privileged have an inherent incentive to undercontribute to cleaning up the environment because they will not be the most benefited by such collective action. Another way of saying this is that the more affluent and developed, acting out of self-interest, have every incentive to maintain the status quo because the damage from their lifestyles are accruing to someone else.

Consistent with the way collective action has been framed in this book (which is not the only way to frame it), it helps to understand the issue of environmental injustice as stemming from the radical separation of self from the other. Pulido (2015) develops this thesis in terms of Spivak's (2003) notion of the subaltern, suggesting that these environmental injustices are possible because the privilege of some, and the subaltern status of others, have been normalized by society. The subaltern is one who has no voice and is perceived as a lesser being (or reduced to an object

---

[2] A useful comprehensive treatment of environmental justice, mainly focused on the US, can be found in Sze (2020). A more global perspective can be found in Natarajan (2021).

category). But it stems from disconnectedness, the alienation of self from other that results in an accepted norm that the other is different. The other's communities are liminal, minority, underdeveloped, and dissimilar. To live in these communities or these countries means living in lesser conditions and, closely following upon this logic, for someone living in these places to be of lesser worth.

Responding to systematic, cumulative burdening of some communities requires multiple and overlapping strategies – some communities adopt Alinskyite strategies for protest and legal challenge, while others more Freirean approaches for critical reflection (Gonzalez & Lejano, 2007). But there is room for other strategies such as discussed above, where we strive to reconnect the disconnected. Writing about environmental injustice in the US, Sze reflects: "Feeling for other beings can lead us away from the death cult of whiteness, carbon addiction, and capitalism... This empathy has been in far too short supply, embedded as we are in the political and economic systems that structure our lives," (Sze, 2020, 101).

This means making the conditions under which the other lives more tangible and immediate. More than this, it means introducing the other in authentic ways, seeing their face, and hearing their voice. It means making sure that no one in a city is invisible. For example, some have developed curricula centered around building empathy through the encounter of the stories of others (e.g., Witt, 2016). Others use media to create digital stories for dissemination through social media (e.g., Gladwin, 2020). Lu (2021) tested the identifiable victim effect in the context of environmental injustice. Specifically, Lu tested responses to appeals for collective action for environmental justice and found higher levels of engagement among groups who had been shown the picture of one of the victims (a boy suffering from respiratory ailments from the pollution). Advocates for social justice increasingly use personal testimonies from victims of environmental injustice to bring a face and a voice to legal proceedings.[3]

It may help the reader to think of relationality as a dialectic between connectedness and disconnectedness, or two sides of the coin, with sustainability

---

[3] These strategies are crucial but it is nevertheless an uphill battle. Stokols (2018) recounts a public hearing on the Chiquita landfill, in the County of Los Angeles, California, where community organizations invited beleaguered residents and environmental professionals to provide testimony on the harmful effects of the landfill. At the end of the testimonies (as recounted to the author by an attendee), a county supervisor proceeded to read a statement (evidently pre-prepared even prior to hearing testimonies) approving the cancellation of the landfill closure and extension of its operating permit. Even when community speaks, it is often not even heard.

on one side and environmental injustice on the other. Perhaps the most succinct way of framing relationality is about the distance between self and other and how such relationship can heal or hurt.

4.6 IMPLICATIONS FOR PRACTICE: EDUCATING FOR EMPATHY

If relationality is a fundamental feature of the human condition, then we should take it into account in the many arrangements we make to structure our everyday lives. We need more effective strategies to activate empathy and, in so doing, promote pro-social and pro-environmental attitudes and behavior. We don't mean to try to manipulate people into caring. First of all, caring may not be something manipulable. Secondly, manipulation is unethical. There is a literature decrying the practice, in some organizations, of such manipulation, such as when some development organizations sensationalize poverty (e.g., see Sontag, 2004; Fischer, 2014). What we mean is enabling people to discover and make connections with the other that is authentic and that responds to people's needs for such connectedness.

In this section, we examine some everyday institutions where a renewed focus on empathy would serve society well. One is education. After all, if the need to relate is a basic human condition, then perhaps the field of education can give some space to fostering people's capacities to relate with the other. Some institutions are becoming increasingly aware of the need to foster empathy among children.[4]

Giving children many opportunities to encounter the nonhuman other is a route to fostering environmentalism. Zoos and museums are perfect nonformal classrooms (Schwan, Grajal, & Lewalter, 2014). In the box shown below, we show one particular organization which has adopted a number of basic strategies in their nonformal education program. These same strategies are relevant to the classroom setting as well, where students can learn about, and be open to, the other (whether human or nonhuman).

Fostering Empathy at the Woodland Park Zoo

The following are some of the practices used by one particular zoo to foster empathy among visitors, and the text below are taken directly from the zoo's Best Practices Framework (Woodland Park Zoo, 2019).

---

[4] A related literature focuses on the connection between one's sense of the interdependence of beings and nature and pro-environmental behavior (Hernández et al., 2012).

INTRODUCING THE ANIMAL

- Use personal pronouns and individual names. Names are powerful indicators of sentience and individual value. "It's a brown bear" implies he's an inanimate object, but "his name is Denali, and he's a brown bear," tells us he is a someone.
- Give people the individual age or personal traits of an animal, if you know them. These help individualize the animals even more than talking about a species as a whole.
- Be accurate and productive when providing information. People are prone to project their own emotions (and sympathize) rather than empathize with another's true perspective. Make sure to give correct information that will help people connect to animals, but be mindful of what you are saying since we do not want to promote misconceptions.

Informing Our Audience

- Tell a story. The most effective empathy-evoking stories are ones that highlight an animal's relationships and an animal's choice and sense of agency. For example, "Taj and Glenn, our greater one-horned rhinos, love taking warm showers. We found out one day that the hot water heater was broken because they refused to take a shower. We fixed it immediately, and they started taking showers again..." is much more compelling than "rhinos like being in water." This shows the animals' choices, as well as our efforts to provide the best animal welfare.
- Provide personal facts and natural history facts. Include facts about an animal's way of sensing and acting, common misconceptions, and how they are similar or different to humans.
- Avoid reinforcing fear or disgust. It is okay to acknowledge another person's fear or disgust, be it is better to focus on something else, like a unique fact about the animal they maybe curious to hear.

INVITING PERSPECTIVE-TAKING

- Give the guest an opportunity to observe the animal. Taking the time to observe an animal gives people the ability to learn more and try to imagine what it is like to be that animal. "Notice how he

> is flicking his forked tongue out. What do you think he is smelling right now?"
> – If safe and appropriate, encourage mimicry, storytelling, and role-playing. This is especially great to engage younger audiences and have them take the perspective of another animal.

In her book, Educating for Empathy, Mirra describes how teachers might use the classroom (in the context of the English Literary Arts curriculum) for students to begin engaging with the other. She recommends employing learning approaches that involve critical reflection and perspective taking. The curriculum needs connected learning, in which where students use digital tools to connect with peers outside the school (Mirra, 2018). Mirra describes strategies for increasing the student's level of civic engagement, promoting a service learning orientation to education that is neglected in current initiatives at educational reform (especially in the test-based regime of US K-12 education). Pedagogic techniques such as participatory action research can be learned in the classroom and then applied in the field. In a five week service-learning project among 1st, 2nd, and 5th grade schoolers, Scott and Graham (2015) found an increase in measures of empathy and civic engagement post-intervention. The arts can also be a pedagogic tool – Athanases and Sanchez (2020) discuss how teachers can use drama in the classroom, such as reenacting historical events, to foster in perspective taking. Role play, especially in the context of moral dilemmas, is another pedagogic strategy (Upright, 2002).

Connecting Students, Building Empathy

How do we use connectedness to foster caring? One organization, Empatico, had a vision for fostering empathy by digitally connecting classrooms around the world. Empatico offers a free digital platform that connects children around the world through virtual exchanges to build relationships, deepen empathy, and bring learning to life. They provide an all-in-one video conferencing platform (compatible with in-person, remote, and hybrid learning environments) where K-8 teachers can find a partner classroom elsewhere in the world to hold joint classes and have their students partake in fun activities to get to know each other and explore a variety of topics together (such as, food, local landmarks, books, and more).

Empatico's mission is to create a more empathetic future generation by connecting classrooms around the world. Empatico enables children to experience meaningful connections by discovering how their peers live and empowering them to recognize and appreciate their shared humanity. Their website encourages teachers and their students to "Take an international field trip, no passport needed."*

The creators of the platform clearly built their philosophy around the idea of empathy through connection. They offer a library of both in-classroom and virtual exchange activities, all designed to foster empathy across a variety of topics and prepare students to meet peers from different parts of the world. The respectful communication and perspective taking guides include role play and reading stories to help students master these skills. The library also provides resources to support educators in their journey to foster empathy using Empatico and beyond.

On their website, one can listen to teachers sharing their experiences. Wendy from Delaware, USA, and Oluwaseu from Lagos, Nigeria, talk about how their classrooms encountered one another's and the effect it had on their students' social-emotional growth, and how the two teachers developed a friendship in the process.

The power of connection goes beyond the useful metrics used in classrooms. But evaluation is possible and should be done more frequently. In 2018–2019, the Empatico team did just that and compared learning outcomes between classrooms that had participated in the Empatico virtual exchange program and control groups that had not. They found significant increases in measures of cognitive empathy (perspective-taking) and perceived commonality with children from other countries (Empatico, 2019). They also assessed their joint program with the World's Largest Lesson, where educators and their students were introduced to the United Nations' Sustainable Development Goals and shared how they could take action to achieve them. They found positive effects, which pointed to students increased awareness of the SDGs and interest in taking action.

*https://why.empatico.org/ accessed June 30, 2021.

Every child should have a pet. Of course, not every family will have the space or other resources for pets. But, even here, there are possibilities for encounter. Can we imagine pet-friendly institutions, especially schools, where people are free to have their pets accompany them? Such a practice would allow children in schools to have some engagement with pets on a daily basis. Could we have officially pet-friendly universities? Could we have more pet-friendly offices, stores, etc.? Could cities strategize around increasing ecological habitat within the city, and also make the city, in general, more friendly to the nonhuman other?

There are many possibilities for increasing connectedness between the human and nonhuman other. For example, the foundation, Animals Asia, runs a volunteer "Dr. Dog" program where owners can sign up their dogs to visit the people in hospitals and senior homes. It is described as an "innovative animal-assisted therapy program that provides people in need with what they need most – a best friend" (Dr Dog, 2021). Yu found statistically significant reductions in level of anxiety, aggressive behavior, and verbally agitative behavior among older persons with dementia after participation in the Dr. Dog program in Hong Kong (Yu, 2014). Researchers have found that such programs have the potential for enriching the lives of the patients (e.g., Curran et al., 2019).[5] The organization also runs a parallel program, called Professor Paws, where dogs visit elementary schools, allowing children to develop familiarity and relationship with canines.

Books can also be a frigate for discovering the other. Storybooks, especially when the main character is an animal, allow the child to wonder what the dog or bird or pig in the story is feeling and experiencing – which is essentially perspective-taking. This applies even when the animal is a fictional one (Hahn & Garrett, 2017).

Another type of (nonformal) education occurs in the world of consumerism. Consider consumers to be like students in the classroom. The classic model of the thick market is one where all the consumer knows and sees, apart from the commodity, is the price. Now, consider the alternative: what if we had a world of informed and connected consumers, who were cognizant of where and how their goods come about, under what conditions they are produced, and who produces them? What if the other behind the commodity were no longer hidden but someone known to the consumer?

---

[5] The logical next step for these evaluations is to also investigate, to whatever extent possible, if the experience is positive for the dogs, as well. Karina O'Carroll, Animal Welfare Education Manager for Dr. Dog, discussed how the welfare of the dogs are foremost priorities of the program.

Marketing can be a tool for education, not just geared toward turning in a profit for the supplier, but educating (and connecting) the buyer. Labeling has been used to increase the connectivities, such as the use of fair trade or sustainable fishing certification (and, more recently, proposals for a carbon footprint eco-label). However, marketing can aspire to so much more.

In this multi-media age, marketing can reveal the hidden life of the consumer good – connecting the buyer to information regarding where it is made, who makes it, what the wages and working conditions are, whether sustainable practices are maintained, and other rich and vital information. In some cases, perhaps the consumer can be directed to the producers themselves. For local area suppliers, farmers' markets are a celebrated way to connect producer and consumer. For more remote sources, people can make a connection through technology. Is this information overload? Perhaps, but it need not be. Sometimes, all it takes is to hear a word, see a picture, think a thought. Given people's rapacious consumption of social media and the knowledge in it (or lack thereof), perhaps information overload is not as big a limitation as one would think.

Take the case of fair-trade coffee. Some organizations provide the potential consumer with information on the growers and the place the coffee is grown in. In some cases, the website provides videos with testimonials from some of these growers. The point is that, whereas the buyer-seller relationship is typically nonexistent, there is the possibility of some kind of connection. Could we imagine enabling even more direct connection, where consumer and producer can actually virtually meet, exchange pleasantries, even get to know one another? In the digitally connected world (accelerated by the COVID-19 pandemic), would it be possible to aspire toward face-to-face encounters like those that occur at a farmer's market? Could we, through different means, simulate the organic connections between producer and consumer that were severed by modern urban life? What was simply a bag of coffee beans, with a price tag, is now endowed with new meaning: these are the beans Leticia and her family grew on their sustainable farm in that beautiful hilltop in Salento. I wonder how they are doing, with the kids attending a new school. Does coffee still give Lucho, her husband, insomnia? This is not simply a bag of coffee among a million other bags of coffee.

Connections can mean much to the consumer. Many will go out of their way to purchase a car from a particular dealer, even when it would cost more there, simply because they know the dealer. Trust certainly is part of this equation, but much more – affinity, loyalty, friendship. To the strict utilitarian, all of these simply appear to be inefficiencies. This is not the way a market is supposed to function. But, do strict utilitarians still exist (have they ever)? In Chapter 6, we look more closely at the issue of institutional design.

Even in sophisticated social network models, where ties are not simply binary variables, the notion of exchange can be reductionistic. In the buyer-seller network, the tie is seen simply an exchange of money (for the good). But, as we have seen, a relationship is a much more complex exchange. It is, as with Levinas, a responding to the other, or as with Gilligan, a giving of self to another. We would each be impoverished (strict utilitarians are free to interpret this in terms of a reduction in utility) were exchanges to be less than this.

Consider the problem of climate change. Sound proposals already exist to make the consequences of fossil fuel use more tangible to the consumer, for example, by linking one's annual consumption to crop or habitat loss, or by carbon footprint eco-labeling. We can go even further. Why not connect the busy urbanite to those who are the first to suffer the ravages of climate change? These are the families who live with desertification, who stand to lose livelihoods or even homesteads. The dire conditions feared by climate activists in the developed countries are already being experienced in some parts of the world. Nonhuman others would suffer in these places. During the tragic wildfires that swept Australia in 2018, many people were much moved by the photographs of kangaroos and other animals displaced and killed by the disaster. Instead of just informing people about the consequences of climate change, we can connect them to the otherwise faceless others who already suffering these consequences. This is not simply marketing. Or, to put it another way, true marketing is not simply about the maximization of consumer and producer surplus. It is allowing people to come back to their authentic selves, realizing that the phenomena of everyday life, including consumption, are wrapped up in the lives of others.

Consider the encouraging rise of social responsible mutual funds in the last decade or so. These funds allow people to invest in securities in companies committed to socially and environmentally responsible practices. It would be even more meaningful if there were ways for potential investors to find out exactly what projects these companies were doing, where, and who were being benefitted by them. Is the "other" on the other end of these activities salient and knowable to us?

The lesson is to seek out, in each collective action situation, concrete ways to reconnect people, animals, and places. The adage about how we need connections is more than a truism; to some extent, we *are* our connections. A digital age where the ability to connect and reconnect is constantly finding new pathways, presenting a world of new possibilities. This is not to say that every connection is a nurturing one. One need only look at the snark found in online blogs or the disinformation in much social media to see that some of these exchanges are actually dehumanizing. However, these are the exceptions that prove the rule. When done faithfully, with sincerity and openness, the encounter with the other can change us and shape who we are for the better.

5

Illustrations

Governing the Commons

In Governing the Commons, Ostrom described a number of long-standing resource management institutions, ranging from the highland meadows of Switzerland to the zanjeras (or irrigation districts) of the Philippines, all of which evolved outside the market and the state. In these descriptions, communities self-organized and developed rules for appropriation of the resources, such as the use of scripts for the right to be included in the rotational access to irrigation water in Valencia, Spain. McGinnis and Ostrom summarize a number of general institutional design conditions that she and colleagues found in these cases, as follows (McGinnis & Ostrom, 1992, 9).

- Clearly defined boundaries of the resource.
- Rules for resource appropriation tailored to the local conditions.
- Collective-choice processes for rulemaking.
- Monitoring appropriation of resource.
- Graduated sanctions.
- Conflict-resolution mechanisms.
- Nested institutions.
- Recognition of right to self-organize.

The last condition relates to the state's willingness to recognize these community-based institutions. All of these conditions are consistent with the basic theory Ostrom laid out in the introduction of her book, which hearkens back to the logic of the repeated game. Central to the logic is the evolution of rules and the ability of community members to sanction violators (recall the tit-for-tat game). While the examples in the book all pertain to formal rules, presumably codified or at least somehow institutionalized, later work by Ostrom and others make it clear that in many cases rules are informal, or as she called them "rules-in-use" (Ostrom et al., 1995). In the world of flesh and blood actors, definitions are blurred, and it is hard to draw the line between what constitutes a rule versus not. For example, social norms can be considered rules, as can moral principles. Cultural practices can be considered rules. Berkes (2017) points to this complexity when he suggests that practices around resources are governed by "action-practice-belief complexes."

As noted earlier, I doubt that any of these researchers would claim that the logic of such resource management derives solely from the utilitarian logic of the repeated game. Ostrom herself makes it clear that mechanisms in the real world are complex and that decisions are driven by "the preferences that individuals have related to benefits for self as well as norms and preferences related to benefits for others" (Ostrom, 2010, 659). However, the strong focus on rulesetting, monitoring, and sanctioning in these works speak to the (implicit or explicit) calculation of material costs versus benefits that each actor has to make in deciding upon what action to take.

Our interest, in this book, is to highlight a pathway to decision-making that is based more on empathy and less on a utilitarian calculus. Now, just as boundaries around what constitutes a rule are blurry, so too, in real situations, differentiating one motivation from another is challenging. People's intentions and actions are guided by many complex motivations. Invariably, institutional models, including Ostrom's earlier work, usually emphasize conditions that lie closer to the individually rational end of the continuum versus the other (Ostrom et al., 1995). In the decades following the publication of Governing the Commons, hundreds of researchers proceeded to conduct remarkable research in the field that uncovered many examples of rule systems, with mechanisms for monitoring and sanction, developed by the community.[1]

In this book, we do not claim that institutions can or should be created solely on the foundation of empathy. Our observation is simply that this mechanism has been underappreciated and under-utilized. Institutional designs (especially that of formal institutions) do not do enough to activate other-regard. An institutional mechanism such as the carbon tax,

---

[1] Pertinent literature focusing on the importance of systems for monitoring and sanction include (Baland & Platteau, 1996; Agrawal & Goyal, 2001; Gibson et al., 2005; Pagdee et al., 2006; Ostrom & Nagendra, 2006; Coleman & Steed, 2009).

in concept, need not require any cognizance of the other at all. With a market-based instrument like a tradeable emissions permit, there is no need to recognize the conditions experienced elsewhere, and by whom, since all one has to know is the price signal. Such policy instruments are designed so that it does not matter if you care for the other (or the environment, future generations, farmers, etc.). The tax or subsidy makes you act the right way, regardless of what or who you care for. Its proponents would say that this instrument works without having to rely on such a soft, unreliable phenomenon such as empathy.

What is lacking with the conventional approach? First, these autonomous instruments may not do enough (Rosenbloom et al., 2020). We may require a wholesale transformation of how we go about things, which may require an internal transformation as well, so that we act in ways beyond where the policy instruments move us to act. Second, a policy mechanism such as a price may not capture what matters the most in this life (e.g., love for your loved ones) so "getting the prices right" always will miss the mark, misallocate resources, and cause actions not completely in accord with what matters to us. Lastly, we repeat, no instrument need act on its own. Empathy can have a large role to play, in conjunction with these other strategies, in moving people to cooperate, go beyond the minimum, and seek new solutions and strategies not encompassed by formal policies. It is one thing to refrain from actions that might harm your neighbor, and another thing to take actions to help and support them. Setting a price on carbon invariably involves, somewhere, somehow, people balancing the costs and benefits of reducing carbon emissions – but invariably the calculus decision-makers use for such trade-offs leave out many of the things most important to us. If the experience of the United States (and other countries) in recent years says anything at all, it is that, when people care only for their ingroup and not for the other, many will experience policies such as carbon mitigation as externally imposed burdens that they will reject (Bertin et al., 2021).

Whether we talk about aquifers, forests, or the atmosphere as a commons, we contend a crucial role is played by connectedness and ensuing empathy. In this chapter, we describe some situations that indicate, at least to some degree, that this mechanism is at work in important ways.

Many situations we face today do exhibit characteristics of the commons that, at the same time, pose challenges for the community-based solutions and design principles that Ostrom advocated. Perhaps there is no larger example of a commons than climate. Framing climate as a commons, we can view carbon use (and emission) as analogous to Hardin's cows on the pasture, where excessive emission of carbon ruins the climate/pasture. However, it is difficult to encompass the climate question within the logic of the repeated game. First, once we exceed the sustainable use of the pasture, there may be no game left to repeat. Second, in the climate game, the violator (our generation) may not face any sanctions from the rest of the community (the next generations) because of the separation in time. Whatever the willingness of people today to self-sanction, it cannot be equivalent to the motivations of the next generations on whom the costs of our carbon use will mostly fall. There are ways to try and remedy these externalities (a time machine would work), but our contention is simple: whatever the solution is to climate change, such a solution will never be complete or even achievable unless we tap into people's capacity for empathy. If this is is true, we have to start thinking about how to promote connectedness, even across the generations.[2]

The literature on the commons has long recognized the importance of social capital and social networks. As Dietz and Henry assert: "All human activity is embedded within social relationships, where interactions continually reshape beliefs, norms and values, and ultimately actions. We know that certain types of governance arrangements, such as collaborative policy-making institutions, may lead to the formation of networks that in turn promote the development of social capital and grease the wheels of altruistic collective action" (2008, 13189). Scholars have yet to unpack how the constellation of relationships in a given place shape the kind and extent of collective action that results. This task is all the more challenging because relationships work in ways that one does not see when examining the structures of social networks (e.g., modeling them as graphs). Just looking at the spatial arrangements of people from plan view, one cannot tell a street fair from a melee. Furthermore, the task is not made any easier by representations of social capital as some kind of banked resource that sits somewhere, waiting to be used for collective action.

---

[2] Many climate advocates believe in the power of relationality without explicitly framing it as such. When people argue that we must care for what the future will look like because these are our children and our children's children and so on, these are relational claims that are founded on empathy of the human for the other. A different, but related, argument is reflected in literature that talks about situations when discount rates should tend toward zero (e.g., Stern, 2006; Broome, 2008).

5.1 RELATIONALITY

We know that in innumerable situations, people's actions vis-a-vis ecology are guided by their relationship with that ecology more than by systems of rules. In his book, Sacred Ecology, Berkes describes a number of indigenous traditions around ecology in terms of "knowledge-practice-belief complexes" – that is, in local cultural traditions that are not so much codified as sets of rules but internalized as relationships with the other and community (Berkes, 2017; also Berkes, Colding, & Folke, 2000). He gives as an example the Cree of St. James Bay, a hunter-gatherer community. "The Cree say that the main reason for showing respect to animals is that humans and animals are related, they share the same Creator. Just as one respects other persons, one respects animals" (Berkes, 2017, 116). The attitude of respect is an ethic that is imbued in all aspects of relationship with the hunted animal, from the approach to the hunt to consumption. Respect includes not wasting anything and making use of all parts of the game. This includes burial of the remains, with some going to the land, and other remains going to the water as is fitting.

While it is possible to depict such knowledge-practice-belief complexes as systems of rules, at some point, it is clear that it does not suffice to do so. The system of rules is not one of mechanistic (codifiable) standards applied systematically. Rather, it involves a keen sense of balancing conditions and assessing the situation to determine the right course of action. In Berkes' observation of Cree hunting practices, there are innumerable actions guide the harvest (e.g., assessing the fat content of the game, the animal's movements, monitoring the health of the beaver-vegetation system), all guided by the overall principle that the animal, not the human guides the harvest, a striking departure from the anthropocentric world-view. Berkes concludes: "Traditional worldviews of nature are diverse, but many share the belief in a sacred, personal relationship between humans and other living beings... Many indigenous people manage relations with their environment; they do not manage resources..." (Berkes, 2017; 127–128). The idea of a complex system of knowing, believing, and doing emphasizes the multi-dimensional nature of relationship, where it is not just empathy with the other that evolves but also the exchange of knowledge and attitudes from interpersonal relationships within a community.

Perhaps the logic of relationship is most powerful in small, tightly-knit communities where each person can encounter every other community member. Would formalized rule systems, based on more utilitarian modes of reasoning, be required in larger commons? In Chapter 6, where we will we refer to this as the "large-n problem," we argue that relationality may act powerfully even in these situations that involve thousands, or even millions, of people.

There is reason to believe that relationality can work effectively for large commons situations. Over a long period of time, the legendary bison herds of the North American Great Plains maintained their populations, owing to sustainable harvesting practices by the Native American tribes. In Native traditions, what it meant to be human meant being inextricably interrelated with the nonhuman, particularly the bison (Harrod, 2000, 43). This belief led to an ethic that fostered a sustainable practice, at least until the entry of the ecological community into the European fur trade market ushered the downfall of the bison population by the latter part of the nineteenth century (e.g., Taylor, 2007). How can we explain this through the lens of relationality? One possibility is that market relations, built upon the non-relational logic of the market, where buyers and sellers (and bison) are separated from direct encounter with the other, removed the conditions where local knowledge, attitudes of shared coexistence, and empathy could govern (e.g., Lejano & Ingram, 2012). For the Native Americans of the Great Plains, they, the bison, and the other tribes were all part of the place, sharing lives bound up with each other's welfare, understanding each other's experience. For the fur traders and consumers in Europe, the bison and its ecosystem just another commodity market and, if the price was right, they thought nothing about driving the system to extinction.

To the purposive, objectivist logic of the market, contrast the ethic of relationality, heard in the following words from a Native American medicine man:

"We Sioux have a close relationship to the buffalo. He is our brother. We have many legends of buffalo changing themselves into men... According to our belief, the Buffalo Woman who brought us the peace pipe, which is at the center of our religion, was a beautiful maiden, and after she had taught our tribes how to worship with the pipe, she changed herself into a white buffalo calf. So the buffalo is very sacred to us. You can't understand about nature, about the feeling we have toward it, unless you understand how close we were to the buffalo. That animal was almost like a part of ourselves, part of our souls." Lame Deer (Lame Deer & Erdoes, 1972)

The holy man gives a wonderful description of relationality. It is about shrinking the distance between self and other. In his words, we see a fusing of identities, where the bison becomes a part of himself and a part of his soul. You do not understand nature unless you have a relationship with it.

In real-world situations, unlike the conceptual models in Chapter 2, it is not easy to set apart the work of relational versus utilitarian motivations. In the real world, people are not Cartesian (or Kantian) archetypes, and they exhibit multiple motivations in a single action. In some situations, however, we see some or one of these motivations are more at play than others. When do we see the relational dimension governing a commons situation?

(i) Relationality might dominate rational-purposive motivations in situations when there are no formalized rules for resource use. It is also possible many rule-like systems (like social norms) can be active conjunctively with the relational. In some cases, there may be the absence of formal or social sanctions for those who act in noncooperative ways. When no (formal or informal) penalties or social pressures exist, then people can act noncooperatively (even illicitly violate social norms) without decreasing their utility.

(ii) We may also see empathy driven relationality most clearly is when actors' actions already meet social norms or formal requirements (so sanctions no longer apply) and then proceed to go beyond them, exhibiting altruistic behavior. In some of these cases, such altruistic behavior might still provide individual benefits in the form of social status or other incentives, but there will be situations when these extraneous benefits clearly don't exist.

(iii) In another type of situation, there are established systems for governing a commons, whether market-based or state-based, yet local actors agree to practice an alternative system outside these formal arrangements. In these cases, we see a different motivational logic at work, inasmuch as the formalized arrangements would represent conventional rational resource use.

(iv) Lastly, we may find relational motivations dominating in some very large-n situations. In these cases, including when the commons is so large as to make it impossible to delineate it, set boundaries, and institute a system of governance, there may be no solution other than relational, empathy-based motivations. Pro-social consumer behavior is one such case (e.g., reducing personal resource consumption).

Recent times have seen the growth of nontraditional commons situations. A good example is the knowledge commons (e.g., see Hess & Ostrom, 2005; Hofmoki, 2010; Frischmann, Madison, & Strandburg, 2014; Morell, 2014) which, while sharing commonalities, differs from natural resource commons in significant ways. For example, particularly with online spaces, establishing boundaries and excluding outsiders may not be feasible. Monitoring and sanction, similarly, may not be possible. In many such situations, relationality can be an important mechanism for commons governance.

Note: the caveats we may harbor about the work of relationality in the real world parallel the caveats we should harbor about the presence of rational modes of reasoning. In each one of the commons examples that Ostrom and colleagues studied, where rule-systems and social or other sanctions were at work, one cannot rule out the parallel influence of relationships, empathy, and altruism. Nor can the success of these governance arrangements be solely attributed to these rational arrangements. For example, analyzing twenty-four case studies in Europe, De Moor et al., (2021) found sanctions to be missing or inconsequential to the successful management of the commons.

5.2 BRIEF EXAMPLES

Some commons may be small enough that most, if not all, of its members, encounter each other. In such a setting, we might hypothesize that relationships will dominate over rational systems of governance. First, as the new institutionalists pointed out, formal institution-building does not occur when the potential gains from formal organization are small or, at least smaller than transaction costs (Williamson, 1985). Secondly, the community can be small enough that interpersonal relationships provide all the coordination needed. If this is the case, then the logic of governance in this system will greatly depend on these relationships.

Urban community gardens may provide an example of this. These gardens most often require volunteer work from residents in the area, and cooperation is even important for harvesting the fruits of the collective labor. It may be the case that some urban gardens are managed like private property, where each resident gets an affixed portion of the property – something like privatization. But in many cases, urban gardens are a collective effort on a collective piece of land that is not parceled out to individuals.

In a study of urban gardens in Germany, Feinberg, Rohgani, and Rogge (2021) found that rules were not well established and that sanctions were not an important predictor of the sustainability of collective action. Rather, they concluded that interpersonal trust was the key factor behind positive outcomes. This echoed the findings of Rogge et al.,

(2018), which also suggested that trust was a more important variable than sanctioning. In fact, sanctioning may in some cases impede trust. The relevant question is: what establishes trust? Most of all, trust requires personal encounter with the other – in fact, something akin to an interpersonal history (Schilke, Reimann, & Cook, 2021, 245). More than the dissociated nature of an abstract social norm, trust implies interpersonal encounter and, in fact, relationship. Researchers find collective action to be positively associated with trust (e.g., see Brugnach et al., 2021 for an exploration of trust and relationship in a water resource game).

Trust can transform the games discussed in Chapter 2, as researchers have found. Commons research shows trust to have a transformative effect on the management of common-pool resources (e.g., van Klingeren & de Graaf, 2021). If trust is such a vital institutional element in cooperation, it would seem that we might pay more attention to it. More than anything else, it is a relational concept. "Trust is a feature of relationships of individuals, of organisations and of institutions that affects their interactions in a supporting way" (Bouckaert, 2012, 94). What is trust? Most often, the literature on collective action defines trust as the belief or knowledge that the other will reciprocate one's own cooperative behavior (e.g., Poteete et al., 2010, 227). However, there may be other aspects to trust; for example, having some idea of who the other is, and whether the other is a person worthy of one's filiation. In any case, it is evident that connectedness can foster trust (as well as erode it), and trust can be more than just reputational.

For now, we simply acknowledge the important role of trust, which needs to be more fully explored, in the governance of the commons. Trust is one dimension among many relational factors as Poteete et al., point out: "Whether the individuals who are interacting know one another, communicate, trust one another to cooperate, and have accurate information about the situation they are in, all affect the likelihood that individuals will cooperate in a dilemma situation..." (Poteete et al., 2010, 216).

Perhaps the logic of the community garden is not altogether new. Moreover, this logic may hold even in some larger systems. In an historical study of European (Dutch, Spanish, and English) commons that lasted more than 300 years, De Moore et al., (2016) concluded that sanctions were not associated with the success and longevity of these non-privatized lands. Rather, they posited that regular community meetings, information exchange, mutual monitoring, and the internalization of norms were the main factors. They suggested that the act of meeting together regularly, sharing ideas and norms, more than monitoring and sanctioning per se, creates for sustainable collective arrangements (see also De Moore & Tukker, 2015). In other words, longstanding commons survived on the strength of relationship-building and relationship-maintenance.

We also find new, emergent modes of self-organized cooperatives that can be understood as a commons. Many online communities constitute a commons of sorts. Wikipedia is a resource accessible to potentially anyone with access to a free, uncensored internet and, so, is a nonexcludable good. It can also be a rival good for contributors, as one's contribution can supplant or preclude another's. Moreover, there are violations of wise use of the resource, as some contributors may post spurious information. A resource like this is thus essentially a commons governed neither by any formal state-centered nor market-based institution. These emergent forms of self-organization come about because the people who join share some common interests or ethics. There may be a feeling of kinship among these memberships and, so, we might suspect that relational mechanisms may be at work in them. Bradley and Pargman (2017) describe so-called new sharing economies as forms of commons. They describe two such initiatives: Bike Kitchen, which is a DIY nonprofit bike repair studio, and Hoffice, which is a "pop-up" commons, in which private kitchens are transformed into one-day shared office spaces for community members. Bradley and Pargman observe that, despite there being no formal monitoring or sanctions (and, beyond general principles, there may be no formalized rules either), these communities operate harmoniously, and members tend to behave in cooperative ways.

5.3 LAB-IN-THE-FIELD

In everyday situations, relational mechanisms are at work alongside formal institutions (i.e., market, regulatory, common-pool resource, and other situations). If it is challenging to find real-world situations where we can study relational mechanisms in isolation, perhaps one can conduct experiments within these situations that do. Some researchers have taken to studying how people situated in their everyday contexts make decisions (e.g., see Janssen & Anderies, 2011 for an overview). We might refer to these as labs-in-the-field.

In a series of experiments-in-the-field, Czap and colleagues created conditions where resource users (e.g., farmers) were encouraged to perform perspective-taking to envision how their actions affect the welfare of others. Comparing behavior before and after this exercise, they were able to assess how empathy (and, correlative to this, relationship) works in field settings. The Conservation Stewardship Program involves a voluntary commitment by farmers to engage in conservation practices beyond what was required by law. In a field experiment, messages encouraged farmers to consider the perspective of their neighbors, wildlife, and future generations who would be affected by land degradation (Czap et al., 2019, 133). The result was a significant increase in sign ups compared to the experiment with a non-perspective-taking message. The increase was greatest when the appeal was made with a personalized, hand-written note. This is exactly what the idea of relationality is about, which is increasing connectedness and empathy.

A similar experiment was conducted by Ortiz-Riomalo et al., (2021) among farmers in the Andean region of Peru. The ecological system consisted of a watershed with upstream farmers engaging in conservation measures to protect water quality, which then benefited farmers downstream. In this case, the upstream farmers were more disadvantaged economically because they dealt with poorer agricultural conditions and poorer access to markets. To aid farms upstream, a farmer's market was created to increase their market access. In the experiment, the researchers asked downstream farmers to contribute towards the farmers market. The control group was given an informational appeal, while the test group had both information and instructions to take the perspective of the upstream farmers. Contributions in the test group were found to be 1.37 times those in the control. Controlling for other factors, the researchers concluded that the most probable driving force behind these contributions was the triggering of other-regard.

In an experiment that lay somewhere in between field and laboratory, Peth et al., (2018) asked German farmers about their willingness to engage in practices that minimized fertilizer contamination of nearby water bodies. They found the voluntary level of commitment to be greatest in response to empathy-inducing messages. The effect was less with messages that involved invoking social norms.

The promotion of cognitive empathy among resource users is a diffused mechanism for encouraging resource conservation, in a way that works even when formal institutions are insufficient for the task. This technique is called "empathy conservation" – that is, using cues and nudges to encourage perspective-taking on the part of the target population. Czap et al., recommend this strategy in conjunction with financial and other incentives to conservation (Czap et al., 2015).

5.4 RELATIONALITY IN THE FIELD

Scholars of collaborative resource management have observed that repeated interaction among policy actors can foster collective action even in the face of conflicting interests (e.g., Schneider et al., 2003; Gerlak & Heikkila, 2007). What is repeated interaction, however, if not the establishing of relationship?

Though connectedness and empathy undoubtedly play an important (though underappreciated) role in the field of real commons situations, almost all situations bring to the fore multiple pathways to cooperative action (empathy, but also the working of rule systems, social norms, and egoistic motives). Still, we can find cases where relational phenomena are more clearly highlighted. For example, studying farmers in a watershed in the US Midwest, researchers found that farmers who scored higher on the empathy/sympathy scale were more likely to voluntarily use conservation best practices (Sheeder & Lynne, 2011).

In some cases, formal monitoring and sanction may even work against (or "crowd out") internal motivations toward cooperative action. For example, Gatiso et al., (2015) observed that, during normal times when resources are relatively abundant, sanctioning reduced the level of conservation of trees in a communally managed forest in Ethiopia. However, community members were more responsive to sanctions during times of scarcity. Aksoy and Palma (2019) noticed an increase in altruism (for in-group, which they define as members of the community) during periods of abundance, but no in-group beneficence during scarcity, which they attribute to the lesser role of socio-cultural effects during extreme distress.

In some situations, formal systems of governing a commons are in place, but local actors practice an altogether different system. In these cases, we might think of relationality as a dynamic that works in the backstages of the formal program or institution (Lejano & Kan, 2022a).

Take the case of the Turtle Islands of Tawi-Tawi, Philippines, one of the world's most important breeding grounds for hawksbill and olive ridley turtles – early accounts described beaches teeming with turtle nests (e.g., Domantay, 1953). Beginning in the 1990s, the government sent biologists and conservation specialists to set up a formal system of turtle habitat protection, monitoring of turtle nests, and sanctioning egg harvesting. Limited egg harvesting was allowed through a permit system that ensured that the major portion of the eggs would be untouched.

Yet, when researchers (Lejano & Ingram, 2009) studied the system a decade later and interviewed some of the conservationist wardens involved, they found a different practice altogether. They would actually allow local islanders to periodically harvest some eggs. Why? In the words of one of the biologists:

"We would know when we were going to get hit [by poaching] ... first, when we hear that there is an upcoming wedding, and you sometimes just need to turn a blind eye...and another is during the Hari Raya Puasa [involving the return to one's place of origin] when they need to find funds for travel...you learn to understand the culture, their dilemmas."

Behind the formal rules, there existed practices that did not conform to any rules but consisted in a fine adjustment of actions and attitudes to that of the islanders. The warden described how he and his fellow conservationists would do a subtle dancing around the presence of the islanders on the conservation site, so as not to apprehend anyone.

"We have three pocket beaches... and my favorite pastime was to vocalize... like this (demonstrates). I would project to the two other beaches, I would have to hear three echoes. In the context of our negotiated presence, they would know I was approaching, because I would project my voice, and they could then hide, so I would not see anyone when I patroled, whether they were there or not... I could not catch anyone in the act, because if I did, I would have to catch you... But I can't catch. I have to patrol, and I've done my part, but we allow a small opportunity, that they can exploit only for weddings, Hariraya, etc."

When asked why an alternative system of governance arose, the conservation wardens interviewed replied that this was simply a part of belonging to the islands. Although they first entered the scene as outsiders, they slowly began to become part of the place, entering into relationships with local islanders in everyday instances. This is a relational logic.

The web of relationships included non-humans as well. In the words of one of the islanders, talking about the turtles (called *pawikan*, in Tagalog):

"We feel for the the pawikan. They help us a lot, in fact, they have given us a livelihood, on our three islands. Permitees (for harvesting) are given a livelihood. ...For us, we see the pawikan as like our children. Because it's just as hard to raise pawikan. ... A lot of the pawikan die. There are illegal fish nets, and illegal trawlers. The trawlers catch them. ... When you look into their eyes [the pawikan], it's as if they are crying. You will feel for them. The same when you hold them... We teach [the residents] how to take care of the pawikan, they should care for them since the pawikan help them."

These words speak to relationality. They help us understand how the entire ecosystem, humans and nonhumans, fitted together. In the case of the Turtle Islands, empathy existed for the "other" in the form of settlers on the island, visitors, and the pawikan themselves. This attitude may help explain how and why the islanders and the turtles coexisted sustainably for many decades. This is not the talk of rules and sanctions but, rather, of empathy and kinship with the other (including the non-human other). One of the biologists described what it meant to work on the islands in the following way:

"The way I see it, because I mingle with people, because I meet people when I go from island to island, people seem to respect me... no, it's closer to something like family, no? ...I go around in jeans, in a t-shirt, or a jacket, little by little, I see people starting to dress like me... I like Ma'am A's clothes, they would say... One really starts to belong. Whatever their custom is, that's what I find myself doing... if they invite me to the fiesta or a party, I go even if I'm not in the mood. When I'm there, people come by and give me fruit, so at some point I would feel obliged to bring gifts, too. But they told me, there is a Muslim custom that says you should not reciprocate the giving of a gift, it's not an exchange. When someone gives you a gift, do not give a gift in return... It's like you did not appreciate their gift enough. ...So I am really at ease with them... when they eat with their hands, I eat with my hands. ...One day, someone came, with the flu... you know, the one pill I gave, they would pay me back with five kilograms of fish. What I mean is, they respect you."

"So, if you don't have a bond with these people, if you don't have a concern for them, apart from your program, you have no business being with them, you might not stay there more than two weeks. They were hesitant with me at first, but now when I am there, we are family. But like relationships with other people, even my own family, you cannot share everything... A limitation is I don't want to tread too much on their lives, and I don't want them to overindulge with me. These limitations, like respect, you always have to maintain these. Although you bond, there is still the maintaining of respect."

The biologists quickly realized that functioning in this environment involved much more than the setting of boundaries, rules, and authorities. It meant becoming part of the islands and embedding themselves in a web of relationships. The blurring of rules and roles reflects a relational ethic. This is why patrolling the beaches could not be done according to code and why the government edict of strict conservation was not followed. Demarcating resource boundaries is not a linear exercise, as the lines between formal and informal, resource and community, blur as well.

"When we talk with islanders there, we talk about how, when we say 'sanctuary', we don't mean just the pawikan, but also the people. We just have to assign, just as with our fishing, limits to what we people do. With the pawikan too, they have their limits, which is what sanctuary means. We could not have a sanctuary and say, leave this place, this is for turtles only. This is what we tell people who help us.

You are part of the sanctuary... In the beginning, there were few people on the islands. One could say, the people were there, and the pawikan were there. But there are a lot more people now. Now, the people and the pawikan have to share the place. It is not anymore one or the other. Now they have to live together."

During the period when this alternative system was practiced, egg conservation actually increased (Lejano et al., 2007). It subsequently dropped, in 2001, when the national government stepped in, abandoning the Pawikan program and classifying the islands with the egg habitat as marine sanctuaries (absolutely prohibiting its use by islanders). Ironically, this formalization of the new conservation program resulted in a precipitous decline in egg conservation activity, reverting to what might be understood as a tragedy of the commons.

How do we understand the undoing of the system? The Pawikan program, formally a system of strict monitoring and sanction, evolved into a finely balanced web or relationships, involving a subtle dance between islanders, conservationists, and the turtles. Governing the working of relationships was empathy. A deep way of understanding the conservationists" attitude toward the islanders and the islanders' attitude toward the turtles is as an ethic of caring for the other. Otherwise, why would the biologists risk their careers by allowing the locals to violate the harvesting rules? And when the government stepped in and declared the entire ecosystem as a marine sanctuary (effectively transferring property rights to the state), this imposition cut through the web of relationships. The commons literature has underscored how community members react negatively to systems imposed upon them by the state or other external agents (Gatiso, Vollan, & Nuppenau, 2015).

Relationships bind humans and nonhumans, as well. In some cases, people can even feel attachment for a place, which is a cognitive emotional bond with one's setting (Altman & Low, 1992).

Place attachment was certainly the phenomenon found among conservationists from the US and Mexico who worked, for more than twenty years, to preserve habitat along the US-Mexico border. They continued to do so despite a lack of success for their longstanding efforts (and even failure, given the fact that the border has become even more impenetrable in recent years). They received little credit for their work, and much personal cost. However, when interviewed, they each (in their own individual terms) attributed their commitment to their attachment to two things: their relationship with other colleagues who had worked with them over the years, and to the place itself (Laird-Benner & Ingram, 2010; Lejano, Ingram, & Ingram, 2013). Place attachment is a kind of relationship, in which the person forms a bond that is closely linked to identity (Proshansky, Fabian, & Kaminoff, 1983). This example underscores the value of trying to assess and describe the relationships that form the foundations of social networks. It may be that the way a program functions, whether it fosters continued collective action or not, is to be found not in analyzing its formal rules and organization but in the relationships that lie behind them. Our analysis foregrounds the relational, with the hope that this approach allows scholars to better explain the functioning of networks in complex situations.

In recent years, scholars have uncovered another important element in the emergence of social networks around environmental action: the role of narrative. Narrative plays an important role in the establishment and working out of relationships among a network's members. Narrative also provides us with a way to access, and even analyze, relationships. We refer to the reader to the chapter addendum for some discussion of this related topic.

5.5 CONCLUSIONS

This chapter does not aim to detract from Ostrom's design principles for managing common-pool resources. We do not want to throw out the dishes with the dishwater. Yet, to focus mainly on these elements of rational design is to neglect an important thing that makes these institutions work – relationships. Rational designs don't necessarily need to put a primacy on efficiency, rewards, sanctions, utility, yet they often do, to the exclusion of much else, that matters: compassion, fidelity, and empathy. Here is the main point of this book: it is the relational that matters the most in governing our interactions with each other and with nature. What is essential is often invisible to the eye.

It is not wrong to think of a natural resource or ecosystem as a system to be managed. The problem is understanding such systems as *only* objects to be managed. Management requires rules, standards, and assigned roles that different actors must play. Resources are assets that need rational allocation, and their extraction must be subject to monitoring and, if needed, sanction. This is the modern way of management (as Weber pointed out). The modernist approach requires the subject to rationally utilize the objects to be managed (think of herders managing their herd of cattle). Yet this is not the only way that we can understand the ecologies on which we depend. We can see these ecologies through the lens of relationality, in which the objects of our gaze are transformed into other beings with whom we relate and interact. The others with whom we establish relationships can include other persons or groups who also depend on the ecology, but they can and should include the nonhuman others too. In an ecological ethic, we're not manipulating things; we're entering into relationships with human and non-human others.

The problem is that, to the professionals and practitioners who manage these systems, empathy, and connectedness seem like "soft" parameters, unlike the nuts and bolts design variables that they use (rules, budgeting, technology, monitoring). How would you institutionalize attachment? People interrelating with each other, sharing selves through their own stories – these are things that policymakers will sometimes acknowledge before they move on to the real matter at hand. However, in these soft, invisible things lies our hope for transforming society and moving past the ideological divide, the gap between first world and other worlds, illusory cultural privilege, and the human domination of nature. It is in the acknowledgment of the other as real, vital, precious, and somehow like ourselves that our efforts to save ourselves and the world should begin and end.

In Chapter 6, we devote some space to the interesting element of institutional design. Ostrom's community-based institutional model came upon the scene as a "third way," which offered an alternative to the regulatory/administrative state and the private market. To which institutional "way" does connectedness and empathy belong?

5.6 CHAPTER ADDENDUM

5.6.1 Narrative, Networks, and Collective Action

Thus far, this book has focused on the direct ties that link an individual to others in a social network. In this empathic connection, we find a chance for individuals to move (cognitively, emotionally, morally) beyond the individual concerns of the ego and into interconnection with the other. Now, there is also the possibility of moving onto the larger scale of the group or community. The linkage to the individual other can expand one's scope of concern to the larger community. For example, developing a concern for a stranded whale can move one to care for the larger issue of marine life and to join a broad marine conservation movement. It is a movement from the immediate connection to a larger whole.

Yet other mechanisms can facilitate this connection to the whole. One mechanism, which we have explored in previous research, involves the role of narrative in forging a social network (which can be a community, an organization, a social movement), which then promotes collective action. In this addendum, we take up the, often vital, role played by narrative.

This investigation began with wondering about environmental conservation programs that persisted despite considerable odds against their lasting (Lejano, Ingram, & Ingram, 2013). One example was the maintenance of a movement for preserving Sonora Desert habitat that spanned and crossed the US-Mexico border. The effort spanned decades and persisted, despite lack of funding, the hardening of the border due to political action, and drug trafficking (Laird Benner & Ingram, 2010).

Other programs have emerged despite antagonisms and institutional roadblocks, such as the evolution of ecological conservation areas in demilitarized zones between opposed forces – for example, the buffer zone separating Greek and Turkish sides on the island of Cyprus (Lejano, 2006).

The research uncovered ways in which the emergence of a narrative or a story about the movement as a whole functioned to establish the group and organize collective action. The narrative worked like the "glue that binds" individuals into the larger movement, giving the collective a sense of meaning of the whole, a sense of structure or organization, and a shared ethical framework. This finding echoes insights from earlier literature on the role of narrative in social movements (e.g., Polletta, 1998; Benford & Snow, 2000). The group and the story reflected each other in intimate ways. The concept we use to describe this phenomenon is the "narrative-network," wherein the narrative and the social network are co-constitutive (Lejano, Ingram, & Ingram, 2013; Ingram, Ingram, & Lejano; 2019; Lejano and Nero, 2020).

The structuring and organizing work of narrative is accomplished through what Ricouer calls emplotment (Ricoeur, 1983), that is, the logical arc that connects otherwise disparate events, characters, and other elements that might be found in, say, a novel. Emplotment works in the real world as well to bind together separate individuals into a coherent whole. In the plot that one finds the meaning of the whole, the ethic that binds the group, and guiding vision that gives direction to the members' individual actions.

In this book, we discuss how connecting with the other opens up one's world to empathize with the other and to act altruistically. Another dynamic that can emerge is the sharing of common norms, beliefs, and practices between individuals – the complex suite of elements that we sum up with the idea of a narrative. Norms and ethics can be conveyed in the form of narrative – in fact, narrative is perhaps the best vehicle for conveying moral considerations (see Nussbaum, 1990). Gilligan formulated her idea of a relational ethic of care on the basis of stories she heard from women who shared with her their process of working through moral dilemmas (Gilligan, 1982).

The linkage of individual to the whole is not about subsuming the person into a group. Just as we talk about relationality as affirming the complexity of the person, the narrative-network also reflects how individuals share in the telling of the narrative. In any group of n individuals, there are at least n narratives, as each person tells her or his side of the story in ways unique but, in other ways, coherent with the way others tell the story. This property, which allows the individuality of stories still to come together and constitute a shared narrative, is called plurivocity (Ricoeur, 1976; Thatchenkery, 1992).

Thus, in a diversity of case studies of conservation in the commons, the research found narrative playing an important role in maintaining and structuring collective action. In the divided island of Cyprus, the narrative of the peace park plays an important role in maintaining cooperation around conservation. The plurivocity of the shared narrative allows different parties, Greeks and Turks, to tell their individual variations of the shared story (Lejano, 2007). Other researchers have discovered the importance of narrative in collaborative environmental management (e.g., Walker, Daniels, & Emborg, 2022).

The construction of narrative is not a separate movement from the establishment of a relationship. As discussed in Lejano (2008), a relationship can be thought of, and analyzed, as a narrative about three constituent dimensions: self, self vis-a-vis other, and self-and-other. The role of narrative in the evolution of a relational identity was described, previously, by scholars like Paul Ricoeur and Jerome Bruner, who described the autobiographical self as a lifelong project of writing a coherent narrative that connects all the disparate pieces that make up one's life into a coherent whole (Bruner, 1987; Ricoeur, 1991). This also holds true for the construction of one's identity in relation to the other. Focusing on narrative helps us understand the evolution of a social network. As each member joins the network, by virtue of connection with at least one other member, the narrative of the group is shared. The narrative contains a constellation of things, including norms, rules, and organizing principles. More importantly, the narrative contains the stuff by which the group's identity is forged. Through the process of diffusion of narrative, the

narrative-network comes into being and the network comes to coordinate its behavior into what we identify as collective action.

Narrative analysis has become an important part of an "interpretive turn" in the policy and public administration scholarship (Bevir &
Rhodes, 2022). Narrative has been used as a vehicle for capturing the
meanings of governance networks, as experienced by network actors
(Dodge, Saz-Carranza, & Ospina, 2019). In this volume, we highlight
the power of narrative in capturing the nature of the ties that bind network members. Just as social network analysis is a way that researchers
quantitatively capture the structure of these ties, narrative analysis can
be thought of as one way to more deeply understanding the relationships
that bind (Lejano & Kan, 2022a). The role of narrative in forging of
relationships and constructing social networks influences how we conduct research, as well. When we try to characterize relationships between
actors, we find that often we end up interviewing these actors with the
aim of getting them to tell their stories. Just as Ricoeur and Bruner might
say that getting someone to describe who they are requires having them
tell their autobiographical narrative, just so we look to narrative to
capture relationships.

The role of narrative in tying the social network together is an open
question and should be the focus of research on social networks and
collective action. There are numerous modes of action by which narrative accomplishes this task. Schon and Rein suggested that groups can
coalesce around a meta-narrative that encompasses individual narratives
and agendas, the implication being that the meta-narrative would exist
on a higher level of abstraction (Schön & Rein, 1994). In recent work,
Lejano and Nero propose that in many cases the meta-narrative is a
foundational (or genetic) plotline that underlies the individual narratives
characterizing each member (Lejano & Nero, 2020). In evaluating how a
climate skeptical agenda was able to attract members from such a diverse
set of social movements (immigration, gun rights, etc.), the researchers
found that all these individual narratives shared a common elemental
plot about the social fracture that occurs when the subject encounters
the alien other. Narrative and framing are powerful lenses for studying
the complex motivations underlying climate action and inaction (Lejano,
2019b; Constantino & Weber, 2021; Hulme, 2021).

These findings suggest another approach to social network analysis,
which is less about uncovering structural properties of the network than
about richly characterizing the relationships that make up the ties that
create it. This approach also raises open questions, such as how to speak

faithfully for the nonhuman other when we try to access that other primarily through human representations (Miele et al., 2015). Narrative analysis is an evolving endeavor. Nevertheless, just as social network analysis has built powerful analytic approaches based on understanding a social network as a graph, narrative analysis strives to understand webs of relationships as stories.

6

Institutional Considerations

Elinor Ostrom characterized community-based governance arrangements as a "third way" of managing resources, differing from the hierarchical logic of the state and the consumerist logic of the market (Ostrom, 1990). At around the same time, organizational theorists (e.g., Powell, 1990) began describing so-called social networks in parallel terms: as a third way of managing transactions, differing from the centrally-controlled decisions and actions that occur within the firm and the decentralized exchanges of the market.

Although they were describing different situations (on the one hand, collaborative natural resource arrangements like communal forests and, on the other, strategic alliances in the corporate world), the parallels between these two lines of research seem strong because, at a broader plane of description, they are describing much the same phenomena in collective action. In either case, positive outcomes are the result neither of privatization nor of an overarching authority directing the actions of individuals. In both cases, these outcomes result from the actions of individuals who, although not bound to act in market- or state-constrained ways, nevertheless can work toward the good of the collective (and the other). The term "social network" is often defined in ways general enough to capture most of the situations described by Ostrom and Powell. As for the behavioral mechanism that motivates actors to act cooperatively, both lines of research ascribe it to similar things, particularly reciprocity. Actors cooperate because they have seen others cooperate who, in turn, saw others cooperate, and so on. After a period of time of mutual cooperation, these actors develop a sense of trust in the other.

Another good way to distinguish these institutional types is to try to locate the locus of control over individual actions. In the market, control in theory rests mostly on the part of the individual. In the hierarchy, ultimately, authority rests in the state or the corporation. How might we characterize the "third way"? Ostrom might describe it as locating control in the network or in community but, in essence, it amounts to individuals acceding to the needs, dictates, and authority of the collective. If the primary motivation to cooperate in the network is reciprocity, with sanctions against uncooperative behavior, then actors will still be furthering their self-interest in this third way, except that, in this case, decisions are made to promote the welfare of the group.

Some researchers have noted the overlapping, or even synonymous, nature of social networks and community-based commons regimes. Work is underway to link the two bodies of literature. The structure of natural resource comanagement arrangements can also be depicted using network approaches (Carlsson & Sandström, 2008). Forms of social capital that are all important to community-based institutions can be understood as a kind of network formation (Burt, 2000).

Researchers have begun studying how the effectiveness of natural resource management regimes can be strongly influenced by structural properties of the social networks involved. For example, highly centralized network actors can play an important role in fostering collective action (e.g., Crona, 2006; Sandström, 2008). The trade-off for centralization, on the other hand, can be marginalization of some actors in the periphery (Ernstson et al., 2009).

The social networks around natural resource management can be complex. What Ostrom and colleagues refer to as a community can be composed of a heterogeneous group of individuals. Social ties among heterogenous groups of actors can be a source of learning and adaptive management (e.g., Lejano & Ingram, 2009; Sandström & Rova, 2009). In many cases, these are cross-scalar as well as polycentric (e.g., Ostrom & Janssen, 2004; Andersson & Ostrom, 2008).

The social network literature has focused most closely on the structure of the network, but what seems to be insufficiently analyzed is the nature of the ties (in our language, relationships) that make up the network. Some network scholars recognize this dynamism. As Bodin and Crona suggest: "We also think it is important to point out that not only the structures of a network can evolve, the content of what is transferred through the ties can also change over time. A relational tie that, initially, is used only for the exchange of some specific kind of

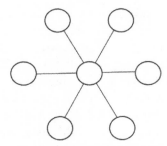

FIGURE 6.1 Example of a centralized social network.

information, e.g., sustainable farming practices, can evolve into deeper social relationships which in turn can facilitate the development of common norms and values" (Bodin & Crona, 2009, 372). In its most typical form, social network analysis constructs a matrix of zero and one entries (i.e., either linked or not linked). However, this does not tell us much about what the nature of the linkage is, how it affects how each member thinks and acts, and how it might possibly work to engender collective action.

But there is one aspect that seems to be rendered more clearly in the social network literature, at least in some part due to its penchant for diagramming network structure. The literature underscores the idea that the network is composed of policy actors (individuals, groups, etc.) linked to each other individually, but not necessarily linked to everyone else in the network. While in the commons literature, there is the somewhat amorphous notion of a "community," the social network literature focuses on the parts as well as the whole. An important idea conveyed by the social network diagram is that a person may be linked to a network by virtue of a (personal or not personal) tie to someone else in the network, but not necessarily linked directly to others. A network can exist even if many of its members have ties to only one other member in the network. For example, in the network diagram shown in Figure 6.1, only one member has ties to more than one other member of the network.

The idea of a social network (even the act of trying to depict its structure with a diagram) is a facile one. It can encompass an infinite variety of configurations, like snowflakes (which are, after all, network diagrams). One can imagine how different networks are linked together, bridging groups across levels of a hierarchy or across scales of governance – what some refer to as polycentric governance (Ostrom, 1999;

Ostrom & Janssen, 2004) and, in the social-ecological literature, cross-scale linkage (Berkes, 2002). The spatial depiction of groups gives social network analysis its power but also constrains it. Some kinds of linkages are just not easy to depict spatially. As some sociologists (notably Bourdieu and Foucault) have noted, sometimes what determines outcomes or processes in society are less the individual nodes but the web of relationships that wraps around them. The linkages are not depictable as network ties – consider Foucault's idea of power as a circulating discourse constituted by knowledge and practice (Foucault, 1980), or Bourdieu's notion of habitus as a field that prefigures relations in society (Bourdieu, 1977). The socio-cultural field that structures people's actions is something that one can depict spatially only in a metaphorical sense, even if you expand the spatial arrangement into a higher topology (Lejano, 2006).

A social network is, first and foremost, a set of relationships that interconnect its members. Research on social networks should focus more closely on the relationships themselves, describe them more thoroughly, and try to relate the functioning and outcomes of the network by tracing these to the constant working and reworking of relationships among network actors. As was suggested elsewhere, "rather than a macroscopic focus on system structure or a microscopic focus on the individual actor, we choose to build our model by focusing on what goes on in the 'space' between actors" (Lejano, 2006, 234).

In our work, we are most interested in the bond that forms between members who become linked in a network. Part of what must happen is (at least) one member gaining an awareness and knowledge of the other. Empathy can involve this type of reasoning, where a person realizes that the other experiences things in relatable ways, to the point of caring for the welfare of the other. At this point, the actor ceases to simply be an individual acting on individual interests. Stated mathematically, the other's good becomes part of a person's decision function.

Relationality is seen not just in people's decision-making but in how they define their identities, as well. As discussed elsewhere (Lejano, 2008), this awareness is not simply a cognitive awareness of but, in part an identification with, the other. A person is not just who she is as an individual, but also who she is vis-a-vis the other and who she is jointly with the other. Identifying with the other can mean identifying with the general collective, as well. It is for this and other related reasons that spatial measures like network density, degree, and centrality in social network analysis, cannot fully explain why collective action emerges.

6.1 DESCRIBING INSTITUTIONS

These considerations bring us to the task of describing institutions that exhibit relationality. The task is a challenging one, owing in part to the difficulty of describing relationships. Social network analysis is useful in highlighting structural properties of networks, showing which actors are linked to whom, and who are most central in the system. There is still, however, the need to enter more deeply into the ties themselves and understand how they function. So, without discarding social network analysis, we seek to complement these structural accounts with a more explicit accounting of the relationships themselves.

In the literature on natural resource management, scholars have made much use of Ostrom's Institutional Analysis and Description (IAD) framework, to describe governance arrangements (e.g., Ostrom et al., 1994; Andersson, 2015). IAD breaks a complex governance system down into sub-systems, referred to as action arenas. Within each arena, the framework describes important actors, their roles, decision points, and the costs and benefits of alternative courses of action (Polski & Ostrom, 2017).

As the IAD approach developed further, its practitioners began richly describing rule-systems that evolved in place, as well as finding dependent variables that seemed to have significant influence in driving the system to effective functioning (Schlager & Cox, 2018). The literature has compiled a large array of possible determinants of effective systems for managing the commons (e.g., Cox et al., 2020). Methods for analyzing processes and variables occupy the entire spectrum (see Poteete et al., 2010 for a summary discussion).

The present work adds to this literature a primary interest not so much in objective descriptions of the system, but more about characterizing the spaces "in between" actors. Relationships may be uni-directional, dyadic, or other. They may be relationships between individuals, between groups, or even between scales and subsystems. The task of complex description of relational ties remains. There are objective ways of describing ties between actors (e.g., measuring frequency of interaction), but often neglected is the phenomenology of these ties – that is, the meaning of these relationships as experienced by these actors.

In Chapter 5, we illustrated this challenge with two examples of relational systems for managing an ecosystem (the Turtle Islands, US-Mexico ecological range). In both cases, the data consisted of narratives, from policy actors themselves, that we analyzed for plot, themes, and literary devices (Lejano, Ingram, & Ingram, 2013). The main reason for this is that, when an informant is asked about their relationship to another (person, animal, thing, or place), they invariably tell a story. It seems that narrative is a primary vehicle for describing the relational. Why? First, the complexity of a relationship often exceeds what can be captured in a diagram or modeled in an input-output function. Second, one's relationship with another is intimately bound up with identity – that is, who I am, who the other is, who we are vis-a-vis each other, and who we are together (Lejano, 2008). Scholars of narrative, particularly Bruner and Ricoeur, maintain that identity is primarily a story that we weave across our lifespans, using the act of emplotment to connect otherwise disparate things, events, and ideas into a more coherent whole (Ricoeur, 1988; Bruner, 2003). In the Addendum to this chapter, there is an extended discussion of the role of narrative in analyzing the relational dimension of institutions.

If we turn our observation to the entire system, however, we should seek to characterize the system as a dynamic and evolving web of relationships. There are ongoing efforts, among institutional scholars, to characterize relational systems – for example, in public administration (Bartel & Turnbull, 2019) and in public policy (Lejano et al., 2018). These efforts include an ongoing objective of explaining the emergent nature of institutions, and how the pattern and nature of relationships in a network drive its functioning and lead to certain policy outcomes. This literature focuses on the specific aspects of relationality that influence the emergence and functioning of public policies and institutions for governance. One account defines relationality as: "the institutional logic by which established patterns of action in the public sphere emerge from the working and reworking of relationships among policy actors" (Lejano, 2021, 366). This suggests that future research should strive to trace institutional processes and outcomes to the working of relationships.

6.2 NETWORK GOVERNANCE

If there is no overarching authority like a state agency to direct the actions of the members of a network, then how does effective coordination come about? Ostrom's IAD model is largely silent on how governance evolves (Geist & Howlett, 2014). Provan & Kenis (2008) posited three modes of governance: through an external body (that comes close to resembling a state), through an internal centralized organization designated by the membership (that comes close to resembling a corporation), and through

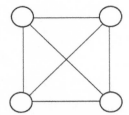

FIGURE 6.2 Complete interconnection.

a diffused system of interpersonal coordination. Of Provan and Kenis' mechanisms, the last one (interpersonal coordination) would seem to be most relevant to our notion of relationality.

As depicted in Figure 6.1, governance can occur through persons who occupy a central niche in the network. In Ostrom's work, case studies involve communities that self-organize and form some type of management structure (with a centralized forum or group where members or their representatives can craft rules of resource use). But when there is no individual or group that can play this centralizing function, the default is the diffused system of many members each coordinating their individual actions. This path of least organization can come about when network size is small (Provan & Kenis, 2008), presumably because it requires close contact among all the members of the network.

Is it necessarily true that diffused interpersonal relationships can create a mode of governance only in small networks? We referred to this in previous chapters as the large-*n* problem. Numerous real-world examples, however, suggest otherwise. As we saw in Chapter 3, charitable causes survive even though donors cannot contact any but a handful of people (and, through media, perhaps directly contact none). Why is this? As Kahneman et al., (1999) suggest, people can feel empathy for an entire group without having contact or knowledge of all the members of the group, through empathy for a single, representative other. Reading about the plight of one struggling child in a war-torn country, a person can be moved by empathy for all such children in that place. This raises the possibility of any of countless variations of interpersonal connections within a network, ranging from networks where every member is connected to everyone else (Figure 6.2) to one where each member is connected to only one or two others (Figure 6.3).

There are other possibilities. Suppose we are talking about a person's use of a resource that causes harms to others (e.g., a farmer polluting a water source). If the resource in question is a pure public good, where

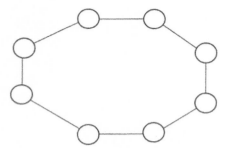

FIGURE 6.3 Sparse interconnections.

one's actions affect everyone the same way, then the logically efficient solution is for the farmer to reduce the harm-causing action to such an extent that the total cost to the farmer is equal to the avoided cost summed up over all the other players. So, if the farmer is connected to just one person in the network and reduces the offending action based on the welfare of just one person, the logical conclusion is that too much of the offending activity will still occur. This is a utilitarian argument, however. From a relational way of thinking, decisions can be made from a different perspective. Recall the simple games discussed in Chapter 2 and the differing decision functions used. For example, one person's reasoning might be something like a satisficing or maximin type rule, where the action is reduced until the impact on the other person is negligible or zero. If pollution in this case were a completely public good, then the farmer keeps reducing the pollution until the impacts to everyone were reduced to negligibly small amounts. In this case, we see that the farmer reduces the polluting activity to a large extent, regardless of how many people she is connected to. Potentially, this can result in more altruistic action than a more utilitarian mode of reasoning. Naturally, if these were private goods, where a farmer's altruistic behavior could be specifically directed only to one beneficiary, then the benefits to society from the farmer helping the other would be less. However, in this chapter, we are talking about the commons where the impacts of the use of some resources are public (or non-excludable).

There are yet other possibilities. A relational logic may, in some cases, eschew the Weberian mode of calculative thinking (Weber, 1920). One can be moved to act toward the good of the other in ways that involve no calculation of costs or benefits. Some can even exhibit a non-consequentialist mode of reasoning, where a person is moved to perform acts of care even though these acts may not *directly* help the other (or at least, not tangibly so).

A person may donate to a charity upon seeing the plight of a child, knowing that the donation might not reach that particular child. In this case, connection with even one other member of a network can lead to altruistic behavior beyond any type of calculative reasoning.

We have yet to discover the full potential of relationality for managing network governance in the commons. In some cases, connectedness and empathy can foster collective action in very disparate, loosely connected networks that are not constrained to one place. Some scholars point to these diffused, global domains as arenas where Ostrom's model, which call for establishing boundaries and access rules, is least applicable (e.g., Araral, 2014). But, regardless of the feasibility of establishing formal communities, relationality requires the person committing to some mode of (ideally direct) connection. As Whatmore (50) suggests: "This understanding of ethical community is relational in concept, insisting on the situatedness of individual and collective efforts to realise new ethical connections and codes and their emergence through the political process rather than some ideal, rational, abstraction."

The insights of the extant social network literature are interesting and important but do not encompass all the possible motivations for altruistic action of one individual for a group. It is possible to imagine networks where some individuals are not even directly linked to any others in the network (such as a person acting solely according to an ethical belief). Although we do not detract from the importance of these phenomena, in this book, our concern is the empathy-inducing effects of connectedness. One's connection to a network may be to a representative member of the network – in this case, the representative member stands in for the rest of the collective group. Moreover, we can define connectedness as encompassing one's connection with a cause, not a being. Some possible ways to amend the network diagram to represent this are shown in Figure 6.4, but seem awkward since diagrams conventionally imitate molecular structures with their pre-quantum-physical "ball-and-stick" representations. Ultimately, the diagrams do not suffice to explain the nature of the ties. The point is that it is difficult to depict the nature of relationality using network diagrams.

The question is: what does it take for the action of a person toward an individual other to also be an action that promotes the welfare of the entire group? What logic governs the function of individuals toward the collective end? In simple cases, it might only require that whatever action is good for a single, individual other is also the same action that helps the group. As discussed, charitable donations are of this nature, since the

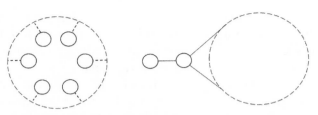

FIGURE 6.4 Alternative representations of networks.

action is the same whether one gives to help the individual or to help the organization that helps this group of individuals. The ties between nodes in a network need not be completely dyadic – in the case of charitable donations, the donor may be moved to give to a needful other, who may be oblivious of the existence of the donor.

In other cases, the nature of the other-regarding actions may be complex, conceivably requiring more complex coordination of one's actions. Mitigating one's carbon footprint can be an example, because weaning away from carbon dependence may require each person to reflect on their lifestyle and make a whole complex set of changes in their daily routine. How does such a complex set of actions evolve across the entire group? Does it require a central authority or source of information, as Provan and Kenis suggest? In some cases, the numerous daily interactions between members of the group may allow a group norm or ethic to evolve. Such a group norm can take on a definite enough shape to loosely coordinate actions of individual members, while not being a centralized edict or codified set of rules. In other cases, as with social media, sharing messages that reach the entire group can allow the group norm to evolve more quickly and efficiently. These norms may not rise to the level of a set of rules. In the language of ethics, these may be more akin to a virtue ethic rather than a deontological one.

The type of coordination that allows a shared sense of right action is sometimes described well by using a narrative depiction of group interactions. Many interactions between members of a network are, after all, conversations or exchanges of text – in other words, people narrating things among each other. Researchers have described how group narratives evolve and begin to coalesce, to the point of coordinating the identity and actions of the network. The social movement literature has long paid attention to the powerful capacity of narrative for organizing a social movement (e.g., Friedman & McAdams, 1992; Benford & Snow, 2000; Polletta, 1998). In the environmental literature, the concept of the narrative-network describes how a narrative and network can co-constitute and mutually define each other (Lejano, Ingram, & Ingram, 2013; Ingram, Ingram, & Lejano, 2019). We can trace how members of the group begin sharing and, telling, a coherent group narrative. At the same time, invariably, each person can tell it in a slightly different way, since each narrator has the freedom to tell their own story the way they see it. This property, called plurivocity, allows each person to tell her story while still being coherent to the larger narrative (or meta-narrative) of the group (Thatchenkery, 1992). There is more discussion of this in the chapter Addendum.

6.3 MECHANISMS FOR FOSTERING RELATIONALITY

A key point of this book is that empathy is an under-utilized "resource." Each human is endowed with the capacity to care, yet society's institutions often alienate people from each other (including nonhuman others). Market institutions are built around a kind of alienation that precludes community-building around collective goods since, first of all, these become private goods. The manner in which goods are exchanged also involve a kind of alienation, as the ideal market functions through streamlined transactions where the "other" is invisible and, in place of the other is simply a price signal (Harvey, 2009). As noted earlier, it is difficult for present-day urbanites to radically shrink their unsustainable ecological footprint (Rees & Wackernagel, 2008) when they no longer have a sense of where their consumer goods come from, who produces them, and under what conditions they are produced. The coffee I purchase online may be produced under conditions of unfair labor, using agricultural practices that harm the environment – I would not know any of this, because all of these "others" are invisible to the transaction, even if I cared.

State-centered arrangements can preclude communitarian action, as well (Deci & Ryan, 1985; Ostrom, 2000). The "other" is just as invisible when people deal primarily with the rules and authorities created by the state. State insitutions are often perceived as faceless bureaucracies and experienced by the public as external impositions that constrain individual welfare. State-centered institutions can impede other-regard in different ways. For example, taxes can crowd out people's willingness to donate to charity. Part of the alienation experienced by people at the hands of the state must be due to the fact that, even when a state body's ends are good, people do not see these ends but only the state. We do not see the good uses to which our taxes are put and do not see the other who benefits from this. We only see the tax, the rule, the imposition.

The point is not to say that solutions to collective action problems that involve the market and/or the state are wrong (or right). Rather, the point is that, perhaps in many situations, our institutions do not tap into our inherent capacity for empathy and other-regarding behavior. One can even say that these institutions are designed to under-utilize these capacities.

We turn our attention to policy instruments, which are the vehicles or mechanisms by which policy is carried out (e.g., see Howlett et al., 2018; also Villamayor-Tomas et al., 2019). Instruments include regulations, incentives, taxes, standards, and other elements of policy design through which the intents of policy are meant to be delivered. Some instruments are procedural, such as requirements for public hearings and public disclosure, and these play important roles in inclusion of different policy actors and their degree of involvement. Howlett describes how procedural policy tools can affect network structure, including information provision and organizing new forums (Howlett, 2015, 87). The following is a preliminary sketch of institutional mechanisms that can be deployed to render the "other" and effects of one's actions on the same no longer invisible.

6.3.1 Informational Mechanisms

Some programs use information-based instruments for environmental protection, but the emphasis has been mainly on the side of the agent of an action (e.g., a polluting factory). Consider the Toxics Release Inventory (TRI), instituted by the US Environmental Protection Agency in 1989, which is a database that lists information about the nature of activity of an industrial polluter. It does not control the polluting activity directly (e.g., through emission standards) but, instead, relies on social and economic pressure to motivate the industry to behave more environmentally. Analyses of toxics emissions of factories in the US right after initiation of the TRI suggests that initial listing of firms in the TRI database did cause a significant drop in their stock prices (Hamilton, 1995).

The policy instruments we envision, however, have more to do with sharing information about the otherwise invisible "other." In the case of the TRI, the other might be the communities suffering from the health impacts of the toxics emissions. Or, in the case of charitable donations to a green fund, the other might be the beneficiaries of the donation – whether the communities where the projects are sited or, more directly, the habitat and species that are helped. Wildlife rescue organizations sometimes feature, on their websites or newsletters, the animals they have restored to health. Dog shelters often provide periodic updates on which dogs they have found and cared for, sometimes giving updates on how they are doing.

6.3.2 Organizational Mechanisms

Another institutional mechanism that has been used (though never framed in the way we do in this book) is that of network construction. All this means is finding new ways, processes, and forums by which individuals and groups who previously had no contact or awareness of each other are now directly linked in some kind of collaborative network. One example is the way water is managed. Often, this is done not by users engaging with each other directly, but through a system of juridical water rights that allocates water across the spectrum of users. During times of drought or other strain on the rights allocations, users negotiate with the state agency and lobby and litigate to increase their share of the water. Yet, in some cases, authorities and stakeholders have begun creating new forums in which the different competing water users get together and interact directly with each other. The now-defunct Cal-FED experiment in California attempted to create a new body for just that (Lejano & Ingram, 2012). Brugnach et al., (2021) have begun investigating how the quality of relationships affects the effectiveness of collaborative forums for water resource management.

6.3.3 Procedural Instruments

Another class of remedies involves institutionalizing new processes (sometimes informal) wherein diverse groups of actors can interact and, in so doing, recognize the other, share perspectives, and move the discussion beyond the fixed positions assumed in many accounts of pluralist politics. An example of such a procedural remedy is the so-called reg-neg process, wherein regulators and key stakeholders meet and negotiate new rules.

The effect of these practices may be indirect, as well. The literature on collaborative governance frames these initiatives as ways by which stakeholders can negotiate new solutions to policy impasse and build consensus, but some scholars also recognize the role of joint activities in simply establishing relationships (Susskind, 2006). These novel institutions are a means for creating new social networks wherein actors form new and authentic connections to one another. Beyond any beneficial effect in the way of consensus-building and resolutions, what this immediately does is to make the "other" real. Whether one sees commonalities or differences with the other, the effect is of understanding the perspective of the other. For this to happen, however, processes need to go beyond completely routinized forums where genuine exchange and discussion tends not to occur. The goal, as some practitioners describe it, should be to go beyond "Robert's rules" onto substantive collaboration (Susskind & Cruikshank, 2006).

It is not an accident that many of these same procedural characteristics have been suggested to be the same active ingredients behind adaptive systems for governance (e.g., Anderies & Janssen, 2013). Indeed, institutional capacities for adaptation and innovation can and should be traced, in part, to the nature and dynamic of the relationships among network actors (Lejano and Kan, 2022a). Similarly, relational analyses can shed light on institutional path dependence and lock-in.

6.4 RELATIONSHIP WITH CONVENTIONAL INSTITUTIONS

Development theory (and practice) has gone through important ideological shifts over the last fifty years or so (a useful summary account can be found in Rapley, 2013). There were important experiments with creating large expert agencies that, in Weberian fashion, built upon a model of the administrative state as a centralized decision-maker. And, then, the pendulum shifted more toward the market – whereas the previous model relied on the state to make decisions regarding infrastructure and services, the market-centered model involved privatizing these functions in a more decentralized form of decision-making that occurs between suppliers and consumers. And, roughly paralleling Ostrom's work on community-based institutions, the pendulum swung again in favor of community, where nongovernmental organizations, neighborhood associations, and other community institutions sought a more bottom-up type of development model. In this book, we examine the possibility of relational mechanisms governing in social networks that may not resemble conventional notions of community.[1] (Perhaps there are social networks whose members share no commonality except for mere interconnectedness.) Are we

---

[1] As described in Curto-Millet and Jiménez (2022), one such example might be the open access digital commons, where rational design principles and resource boundaries may be infeasible.

describing the pendulum swinging once again, this time in the direction of social networks (defined in the most general way as simply interconnected individuals)?

In the previous chapters, we described how relationality might function in a number of situations, where there may be no other formal institutions to link private and collective action. Charitable donations are an example of a diffused institutional mechanism that lies outside state, market, and community. People donate to charity out of empathy for the beneficiaries (although, in some cases, tax deductions may figure into the equation). In these situations, relationality might characterize a distinct mode of governance.

Ostrom's design principles help us identify those situations where establishing conventional institutional mechanisms (including community-centered ones) are not feasible or too costly. For example, the commons (and its users) may be so diffuse that it is not possible to establish boundaries, to identify and assign membership in the commons, and to allocate use rights to the resource. Controlling the release of plastic litter into the world's oceans is such an example. No authority, market, or social network could hope to encompass the universe of sources and the expansive commons involved. In such a situation, our best hope may lie in making the problem, and its effects of sea life, universally recognized (by individuals and governments alike) and developing a shared sense of commitment to keeping the oceans clean. Marine conservation and international organizations have begun using photo and video to make the plight of marine life, dealing with plastic waste, more tangible (Reddy, 2018). In other cases, compassionate behavior is not something that we can hope to encompass with a set of rules (whether codified or not). What does it mean to be compassionate to nonhuman others, beginning with our pets? What does it mean to care? Carol Gilligan did so much to elaborate on an ethics of care, which went beyond principles, rights, and rules but, instead, inhered in compassion, responsiveness, and relationship (Gilligan, 1982; see also Gabriel, 2010).

Yet, in many situations, relationality works in conjunction with conventional institutions for governance, whether they be centered around state, market, or community. Take the case of plastic litter of the oceans. Diffused empathy-driven action on the part of individuals now goes hand-in-hand with formal legal frameworks, such as global treaties like the UN Convention on the Law of the Sea (UNCLOS) and Convention of Migratory Species (CMS), national strategies, and producer-centered programs like Global Eco-Labeling (Thushari & Senevirathna, 2020).

Sometimes, it is too much of a simplification to contrast institutional types as if they were mutually exclusive of each other. Mansbridge points out how Ostrom's community-based systems are often nested within state institutions (Mansbridge, 2014). Similarly, relational systems may exist as part of state, market, or community-based regimes. In this sense, relationality need not be seen as a "fourth way" but something that exists in conjunction with these other institutional models. Stout and Love describe an integrative mode of governance, based on a relational process ontology, where social processes are seen as "coming into existence is an emergent process within interconnected beings and things, as well as the places and groups they co-create" (Stout & Love, 2021, 430).

Relationality can work hand-in-hand with formal institutions and enhance their effectiveness. This is most easily seen in Ostrom's community-centered examples, where strong ties that bond persons to others, persons to nature, and other ties, strengthen the degree of cohesiveness, the shared norms, and cooperative behavior of a community's members. The sense of empathy enhances trust and increases the willingness of members to work for the good of the community and the other. The literature abounds with accounts of strong connections, where members encounter each other face-to-face, fostering highly effective action.

Relationality can also enhance the workings of large formal institutions. The state need not function in an impersonal way, distanced from those governed. Instead, states (through their delegates) can act with compassion, dealing with the governed in ways that are more "person-centered" (Mulgan, 2012). That is, the state does not just set neutral rules but can act in ways responsive to each individual's needs and preferences. When the state does set blanket rules, these can be guided by people's real needs, expressed by the people themselves (Cook & Muir, 2012).

As an aside, the role of relationality in the life of institutions can lead to new directions for policy analysis. While we do not, in this book, dwell on the sub-topic of relationality for policy analysis, this is developed in other work. For example, Lejano and Kan use a play of words, contrasting relational approaches to policy analysis to more conventional rational approaches analyzing how "policy, in its meanings and practice, emerges not just from formal, prescribed rulemaking and institution-building but also from the working and reworking of relationships among a network of policy actors" (Lejano & Kan 2022a, 2).

7

Prospects of Relationality

In this book, we have tried to describe the ineffable, unseen motion of an internal compass navigating barriers of difference in a never-ending search. Maybe, who knows, it is a kind of gravity that, despite the centrifugal forces of alienation, keeps the universe of beings from flying apart.

Relationality is the degree to which individuals understand their being, thought, and action as integrated with that of others and, so, make decisions and take action in ways responding to these relationships. To the degree that individuals recognize and experience an intrinsic connection with others, their thoughts and actions become more responsive to them. This leads us to the following propositions.

1. Relationality, by triggering empathy, can orient individuals (and groups) toward other-oriented collective action.

People can think, feel, and act differently once they experience a connection with the other. Connectedness can mean direct interpersonal connection or even indirect connection or identification with a tangible other. The literature on charitable giving attests to the power of this phenomenon, as there are many situations where identifying recipients of one's giving increases the level of charity. At least some of this is explained by research on the psychology of empathy, which shows how other-regarding behavior is fostered by the experience of identifying with, taking the perspective of, or even witnessing the experience of the other.

Relationality is, of course, not the only route to collective action, but it is perhaps an underappreciated one. This book might be considered an addendum to Elinor Ostrom's ideas about how collective action comes about even apart from the actions of the state or market. Ostrom described how the logic of the repeated game, acting through social monitoring and sanction, motivates actors to act toward collective ends over time. Much literature in the area of experimental games attests to the phenomenon that players exhibit appreciable levels of altruism even in one-shot games where there are no mechanisms for social sanction. Altruism occurs even outside the logic of reciprocity, which underlies the repeated game. Formally, we suggest an alternative, relational model of individual decision-making as one involving vector payoffs where the decision-makers considers others', and not just personal, utility. The book argues that the evidence is strong enough to suggest that relationality, acting through connection and resulting empathy, should be considered as yet another promising mechanism that can promote collective action.

Some of the aforementioned literature point to the effect of reducing social distance in increasing altruism. Importantly, shrinking social distance is not simply equated with homophily, as people are shown to be able to develop empathy for very different others. Seeing pain on the face of another triggers an empathic reaction, even when the other is not like one's self or when the situation is one never experienced by the viewer. The ability to empathize seems to extend to nonhuman others, as well, though some literature suggests that this effect is greater when the nonhuman other is morphologically more like humans. The point is that empathy seems to be broadly applicable in innumerable situations, which speaks to its potential for addressing collective action problems.

2. Relationality can constitute a diffused institutional logic that acts within or apart from formal institutional mechanisms for collective action that involve formal rules, rights, and authorities.

Solutions to collective action problems involve largely formalized rules, rights, and roles. Whether market, state, or community-based, conventional strategies for fostering collective action invariably require specifying conditions for how actors act and penalties for violations of these rules. Ostrom's communitarian model revolves around self-organized community groups who set rules for resource use, mechanisms for monitoring member behavior, and sanctions for rule violation.

Relationality provides yet another mechanism by which collective action can evolve, and it is through motivating the individual's potential for other-regarding behavior – not in response to formal sanctions but largely through caring for the welfare of the other. As we have argued, this capacity for care may increase, in many situations, when a sense of connectedness is enhanced.

There are numerous situations where relationality is employed in deliberate ways. There is a considerable literature on charitable giving, as mentioned above, that demonstrates the effect of connectedness. Charities and environmental nonprofits have consciously made beneficiaries of giving more tangible to the giver. Direct trade initiatives purposely increase connectedness and decrease social and institutional distance to the growers who, in some programs, are seen and heard (through online profiles, videos, and other means). The question now is to what greater use can society make of relationality, deliberately designing it into these and other programs where its potential has been untapped.

In the area of natural resource management, field experiments with resource users suggest that connecting users with others, by encouraging perspective taking or making consequences for others more salient, can increase action oriented towards the collective good. There is also the phenomenon of programs where formal rules are either not active or loosely enforced and, yet, cooperative behavior is maintained. This small (but growing) set of examples suggest that empathy has a role that is not yet fully employed in these situations.

3. There is a need to explore new and more concerted ways to use relational mechanisms to complement conventional approaches toward collective action, especially with issues that call for broad personal commitments.

Whatever role relational mechanisms have played in solving problems of the commons, it has been largely indirect and non-strategic. Such mechanisms are undoubtedly at work everyday, perhaps mostly unnoticed by policymakers. We suggest that the full potential for deliberate employment of relational mechanisms has yet to be tapped.

Perhaps, collective action as formally institutionalized will never be enough in many situations. There is always an other that is impacted in ways greater than most of us. Programs designed upon activating our self-interest may generally fall short of protecting the interests of the most vulnerable. Policies designed for the collective good may have the majority in mind – one recalls the notion, from political theory, that policymakers act in the best interest of the median voter. To care for all, we need to go beyond the "median." There is an inherent dimension of social and environmental justice in problems of the commons, in that policies (and existing levels of action) fall short of protecting the needs and interests of the most impacted. It is particularly in these situations that diffused mechanisms for triggering empathy for the other might be most important.

Looking ahead, we envision how relationality might be deliberately employed in situations that call for diffused mechanisms for engaging people around collective action. There will be situations where conventional mechanisms, such as market solutions or government programs, are just not enough to generate sufficient action, and that broadly diffused personal commitments will matter. In these situations, we call for a more concerted effort to tap into relational mechanisms. We discussed this earlier but will develop these ideas further below, as we illustrate some of the potential for relationality in the area of climate action.

7.2 ILLUSTRATION: DECOUPLING FROM CARBON

Let us illustrate the above propositions by applying them to a specific example, climate change mitigation and adaptation. This issue is a classic problem of collective action, spanning a commons that exceeds any organization, defying the abilities of state, market, or community to address.

7.2.1 The Role of Personal Commitment

While recent developments in the area of climate action have been encouraging, there is a general sentiment among advocates that what governments are currently doing is not enough. Commitments fall short of what is needed to reduce climate change to 1.5 degrees (UNEP, 2021; Meinshausen, 2022). Moreover, actual actions most often fall short of these commitments.[1] There is a sense that much more needs to be done.

If greater efforts are to be taken to reduce and adapt to the effects of climate change, there is undoubtedly a great need to increase commitment, not just on a national level, but on the level of individuals and communities. First, as the climate policy literature underscores, individual commitment is needed in order to support greater government action (Leiserowitz, 2019), and such commitment can entail a sense of responsibility on a personal level (Munson et al., 2021). Secondly, many of the solutions may require action on a personal level, such as increasing use of public transportation or reducing one's energy footprint (Capstick et al., 2014; Dubois et al., 2019).

---

[1] "National climate pledges are too weak to avoid catastrophic warming. Most countries are on track to miss them anyway." Washington Post (online), accessed May 1, 2022 at www.washingtonpost.com/climate-environment/interactive/2021/climate-pledges-cop26/

Yet another consideration is that individuals may need to take action over and beyond what the state (or market) will require of them. States will act mostly with its own nation in mind (Keohane & Victor, 2016). Climate change affects regions differentially, however, and some populations in the developing world will be disproportionately impacted (IPCC, 2022, 14). What this means is that there is an inherent incentive for the developed nations to design policies that under-protect the interests of the most harmed (Warner, 2020). Even more so, global climate policy is dominated by developed nations (Biermann and Möller, 2019), and the IPCC itself is driven mostly by experts and policymakers of (or trained in) these countries (Agarwal, Narain, & Sharma, 2017).

For citizens of the developed world, considerations of justice suggest that there probably is a need to go beyond what their governments, and intergovernmental treaties, are asking of them and to push governments and treaties to go further. There are strong moral arguments for taking action beyond what current international norms are asking for. The most impacted by climate change live in lower-income regions in the world, who also largely were not responsible for the carbon emissions that is spurring climate change (Althor, Watson, & Fuller, 2016). In other words, for most people in the world, there will always be a collective action problem, in that there will always be others who will be more impacted than them. This certainly holds true for questions of justice within generations as well as between generations. Finally, this is certainly true when humans make decisions that affect the fate of billions of nonhuman others (Kapembwa & Wells, 2016). For all these considerations, the role of empathy cannot be understated. Each of us has to imagine the plight of the other, whether in this generation or the next, who would be worse off than we would because of climate change, in order to act beyond what we need to secure our own welfare.

For all the scholarly work around the carbon footprint of society, there needs to be as much attention paid to the *societal footprint of carbon* – that is, the intimate ways that everyday lifestyles are wrapped around carbon, and the degree of collective and social sacrifice that may be required from each of us to decouple from carbon (Lejano & Kan, 2022b). What the transition away from carbon may require of the world's most vulnerable may be too much, and a just transition may call for a greater individual commitment from the more fortunate. People may need to reflect on how their lives are wrapped around carbon and to make a conscious decision to begin decarbonization in their daily round. There is, then, a need for a mechanism that is diffused enough to reach each individual at the most intimate level and engender personal commitment. As we have argued in this book, one such pathway is through empathy.

The relational view sees the interconnectedness of things. In addition to the collective action problem of decarbonization, we should also strive to see the assemblage of actors (which includes carbon) all existing in intimate interconnection. Carbon trading is not simply about moving carbon around. In fact, it can disrupt relationships among people, non-humans, things, and places in ways of life enabled by carbon use.

7.2.2 The Role of Social Distance

In the effort to decouple from carbon, there will be a need for a diffused mechanism for engaging people on a personal basis. This is required both for public support for climate policies but also behavioral changes on the personal level in support of climate action. The literature on pro-environmental behavior is vast, and fostering it vis-a-vis climate action will require strategic action on many fronts. One of them, we suggest, is increasing the personal sense of connectedness with climate change and its impacts.

The idea of connectedness, as a response to issues of the commons, has to do with reducing the radical alienation of self from other. Alienation can stem from disconnectedness along many dimensions – material, cognitive, emotional, but the outcome is that the other becomes for us a lesser being, an object, an invisible entity.

One phenomenon that detracts from personal commitment is the sense that climate is a "distant" problem, removed from one's immediate self and immediate concerns (e.g., Lorenzoni & Pidgeon, 2006; Leiserowitz, 2006). Researchers have begun investigating whether efforts to reduce the sense of psychological distance from climate change might have an effect on motivating greater efforts at supporting and participating in carbon mitigating actions. Van Lange and Huckelba (2021) propose that climate change can be made "closer to the self" through a concerted effort to communicate climate change consequences as more concrete, immediate, and where supported by evidence, more certain. A number of empirical studies have suggested that decreasing psychological distance does have an effect on the sense of urgency of climate action and willingness to engage in such action (e.g., Rabinovich et al., 2009; Spence, Poortinga, & Pidgeon, 2012). Other researchers have found contrary findings, where psychological distance was found to not have a significant effect on climate attitudes or was mediated by other variables (e.g., Brügger, Morton, & Dessai, 2016; Schuldt, Rickard, & Yang, 2018). Keller et al., (2022) conducted a literature review of this topic and concluded that the aim of reaching firmer conclusions was hindered by the complexity and multi-dimensionality of pyschological distance (see also McDonald, Chai, & Newell, 2015; Maiella et al., 2020a).

The concept of distance is many faceted, including spatial, temporal, social, and probabilistic distance (Trope & Liberman, 2010) – these dimensions representing whether climate was perceived as being remote in the sense of distance, far in the future, affecting those removed from self and those associated with self, and being more or less likely to actually occur. Moreover, the literature shows a large variability in how each dimension is operationalized (e.g., temporal distance can vary from the near-future to the distant-future), such that it is difficult to draw stronger conclusions from the literature. Much of the research cited above does suggest that there is potential for psychological distance to be a mechanism for fostering climate action under some circumstances.

The majority of the studies emphasized the spatial and temporal notions of distance than other dimensions, which is a gap in the research considering the potential role of social connectedness in fostering climate action. As discussed in previous chapters, social distance (e.g., the identifiable victim effect) has been shown to be an important factor in areas such as charitable giving for the environment (e.g., Sassenrath et al., 2021). It is reasonable to posit that social distance can be an important vehicle for climate action on a personal level. In some studies investigating multiple dimensions of psychological distance, social distance was seen to be more important than spatial or temporal distance in motivating climate concern and action (e.g., Jones, Hine, & Marks, 2017; Gubler, Brügger, & Eyer, 2019). For example, Stanley et al. (2018) find lowering social distance, in the sense of climate affecting "people like me," to be the strongest determinant (of the different elements of psychological distance) of environmental engagement. Pahl and Bauer (2013) show how taking the perspective of future generations increased environmental engagement. The role of connectedness in fostering climate concern includes the connection to the nonhuman other as well (e.g., Swim & Bloodhart, 2015).

7.2.3 Employing Relational Approaches to Climate

Overcoming the uncertainty and inertia around climate action will have to occur along many fronts. On the side of relationality, some strategies are already taking shape, including the following.

1. Convincing and showing people that climate change affects them directly. Some of these effects will emerge in the future, but some of them are being experienced in their communities even now.

Environmental groups and think tanks have long advocated for greater efforts in making the effects of climate change more tangible to the public. The media have begun participating in this task. Earlier efforts involved a kind of futurism, depicting physical effects of climate change by 2050 or other future date. Al Gore's media piece, An Inconvenient Truth, belonged in this genre. More recent media campaigns revolve around linking effects felt here and now to climate change. Every year, meteorological records are being broken, and media are increasingly linking these to climate change. The basic idea is the same: that the public should see climate change as not just some theoretical proposition, but a reality that can be seen, heard, and felt. People should feel a personal involvement, that they are each personally touched by the phenomenon.

2. Making tangible the greater impacts to others in different times and places. In some parts of the world, some people are already being severely impacted even now. In other parts of the world, the feared impacts are forecast for some decades from now, to be felt by the next generation.

If the IPCC's warnings are borne out, the prospect of a changing climate is worrisome for all. The truth is, however, that for most of us (perhaps most of those reading this book), there will invariably be others who will suffer from climate change to a much greater degree. Some are already undergoing dramatic upheavals in their lives in some parts of the world even now. There is underway efforts to make the plight of the most affected more salient to all.

Media outlets that foreground the plight of the most vulnerable others often implicitly try to deliver a message. One is that, while others bear the brunt of climate change now, these sufferings will arrive at your doorsteps at some point. Global environmental change, through desertification, drought, sea-level rise, or other impact, is creating a mass exodus of refugees (Berchin et al., 2017). Some researchers posit that many instances of exodus from violent conflict have, at their root, environmental degradation (Homer-Dixon, 2010). Through mass migration, their plight disperses throughout the global community.

A closely related message is that of problems that begin in one corner of the world but ripple outwards and, ultimately affect all. The IPCC has linked climate change to the greater likelihood of epidemic outbreaks, and the ongoing experience with COVID has driven home the message that epidemics have no borders. Global price shocks are another type of contagion (e.g., the ongoing escalation in the price of coffee from climate change). The message is that we are all linked, and one's suffering ultimately becomes our own. The other's interests are our own.

Such information can have another embedded message, one that points beyond our direct self-interest. The message is that some will be and are already being greatly harmed by climate change, and it is not just. It can involve an appeal to norms of justice, invoking a deontological argument that everyone has a right to a safe abode and secure livelihood. One is urged to act out of principle. As Carol Gilligan demonstrated, there is yet another kind of ethics at work apart from principles of justice. The ethic of care is something that emerges from the realization that one has a relationship with all others and begins to care.

This approach can combine with messaging that activates other-regard by framing the issue in terms of equity or morality or by including direct appeals to other-regarding preferences. For example, Severson and Coleman (2015) found that an other-regarding frame increased policy support for climate mitigation policies. Similarly, inducing perspective-taking in appeals for climate action can increase engagement (e.g., Pahl & Bauer, 2013). Furthermore, it is encouraging that there is evidence that the positive effect of perspective-taking on empathy extends to nonhuman animals, as well (e.g., Sevillano, Aragonés, & Schultz, 2007; Ladak, 2021).

3. Encouraging social networks around climate action. The idea is that if people are connected to networks of those who are taking progressive action around climate, then norms and practices will diffuse throughout the network.

Connectedness, especially when direct and interpersonal, can involve the dynamic of social learning. We have to learn about climate change and carbon decoupling, and this can come about through social networks. As Vygotsky suggested, sometimes learning does not proceed outwardly with first learning a principle and then expressing it in action, but inwardly, by first taking on actions we mimic from others in our social network and then internalizing the embedded principle (Vygotsky, 1978). There is evidence that shows that social networks (especially among friends) facilitate the diffusion of pro-environmental behavior even apart from the effect of prior environmental attitudes (e.g., Geiger, Swim, & Glenna, 2019).

The formation of social networks around sustainable lifestyles can be a spontaneous, organic phenomenon. But it can also be strategically promoted. There are today, around the world, networks both formal and informal of people beginning to share ideas and practices around reducing carbon footprints.

The measures outlined above are already at work in the world today, but we can imagine how to go about using relationality in even more strategic, imaginative, and concerted ways. Consider the first action mentioned above, which has to do with showing people how their lives are already being affected by climate change. The scientific community has started communicating along these lines – for example, consider ongoing efforts to explain (or conjecture) to what degree recent cataclysmic weather-related events (such as record tropical cyclones or record droughts) can be attributed to climate change (e.g., Reed, Wehner, and Zarzycki, 2022). The popular media has also begun highlighting the connection between recent extreme weather events and climate change.[2]

Consider the second action discussed above, which is making the plight of those already suffering climate change in unprecedented ways more tangible to the rest of the world. We can harness the power of media to bring the faces and voices of the suffering to the rest of us, not in a way that objectifies or romanticizes their suffering, but simply so they and their experience can be more real. One very natural way by which the other makes a connection with us is by sharing their experience with us directly – traditionally, by simply telling their story. Digital media allows people to share their stories across the globe, so we can imagine, alongside the documentaries already being filmed of climate change and its effects, stories of climate change through the eyes and voice of those experiencing it.[3] Even within our own cities and regions, extreme weather events occur that affect some areas and homes disproportionately, and

---

[2] Freedman, A. "In Europe, a historic heat wave is shattering records with astonishing ease, may hasten Arctic melt" The Washington Post online, July 24, 2019 accessed March 1, 2022 at www.washingtonpost.com/weather/2019/07/24/europe-historic-heat-wave-is-shattering-records-with-astonishing-ease-may-hasten-arctic-melt/

Hannam, P. "How bad is this drought and is it caused by climate change?" The Sydney Morning Herald online, accessed March 1, 2022 at www.smh.com.au/environment/climate-change/how-bad-is-this-drought-and-is-it-caused-by-climate-change-20191024-p533xc.html

Ramirez, R. "How the climate crisis is changing hurricanes," CNN online, accessed March 1, 2022 at https://edition.cnn.com/2021/08/21/weather/hurricane-henri-climate-change/index.html

[3] For example, one ongoing project aims to collect videos of survivors of climactic storm surge telling their stories of struggle and survival to the camera –www.environmentalcommunication.space/digitalnarratives

each of us has a chance to visit and witness the impacts and perhaps even get involved in addressing them. As considerable risk communication research attests, for people to consciously act on reducing risks, these risks need to be understood as tangible and personally relevant (e.g., Spence, Poortinga, & Pidgeon, 2012).

Can one form a connection with the future generation, whom one has not seen? We know that one can imagine the other and even take the other's perspective (e.g., Nakagawa & Saijo, 2021). If one can do this for fictional characters (e.g., Batson et al., 2002; Bal & Veltkamp, 2013), then we can do this with regard to the next, nonfictional generation (Pahl & Bauer, 2013). For example, Ferraro and Price (2013) found that appeals for preserving resources for future generations were effective in a water conservation drive. Moreover, one can see the plight of the next generation being experienced by people in some parts of the world today. Like canaries in the mine, some places are the first to experience the effects of desertification, sea-level rise, and other emergent consequences of climate change (e.g., Winerman, 2019.

We can also think of ways to further the third action mentioned above, which is connecting people to networks within which new ideas and actions about climate can be shared. The literature affirms how these networks build climate policy initiatives on a transnational or trans-city level (e.g., Dierwechter & Taufen Wessells, 2013; Kolleck et al., 2017; Lee & Van de Meene, 2012). Social networks can act on a more intimate interpersonal level as well (e.g., Tindall & Piggot, 2015; Cunningham et al., 2016). Networks can bring us to new ideas when we are able to encounter others and see their perspectives. For example, Guilbeault, Becker, and Centola (2018) studied how the participation of US Democrats and Republicans in an egalitarian social network led to both groups converging on how to interpret climate scientific information. Being connected to others in a network fosters perspective-taking and group identity but, undoubtedly, brings about pro-social behavior through other mechanisms as well, such as norm diffusion (e.g., Miller & Prentice, 2016) and information exchange (Shapiro et al., 2020). Tapping into people's innate capacity for other-regard can help address ideological division – for example, Bain et al., (2012) demonstrate how framing climate mitigation as fostering concern for others and interpersonal amity led to increased pro-environmental attitudes in climate deniers. Teodoro, Prell, and Sun (2021) discuss how social learning about climate is amplified in networks characterized by understanding, mutual respect, and influence.

While conventional approaches target people's self-interest, we have discussed how we should pay more attention to strategies that appeal to people's capacity for other regard. Sometimes, the tendency is to choose which one strategy (and corresponding policy instrument) to recommend in a particular situation. Some researchers argue that approaches based on individual utility can crowd out intrinsic tendencies to act for the other (e.g., Rode et al., 2015). It is natural to ask which approach might be most effective. For example, in a review of other-regard and pro-environmental behavior, Heinz and Koessler (2021) found that, of the studies that directly compared other-regarding intervention to self-regarding ones, six studies found a greater effect through the other-regarding route, three favored the self-regarding route, and ten studies found mixed or uncertain results. We should not be surprised to find very different answers depending on the context, since everything is in the detail. There is evidence that multiple approaches, activating different motivational pathways, can complement each other. Ferraro et al., (2011) found that appeals to other-regard had a longer-lasting effect on water conservation when used in conjunction with norm-based appeals. Czap et al., (2015) found that other-regarding approaches were enhanced when combined with financial incentives. In real situations, multiple motivational pathways are activated simultaneously and, often, multiple policy instruments work in concert.

Relational approaches to collective action will invariably work in conjunction with other, more formal approaches. As we discussed, relationality can work behind the scenes to improve the functioning of state, market, and communitarian institutions. Sometimes, relational processes can work separately, in spite the formal approaches (Lejano & Kan, 2022a).

The relational pathway to collective action is one of multiple such pathways that act in concert. We suggest that the strategies mentioned above will be effective in different ways for different people in different contexts. Some people are in a position where normative motivations factor more than relationality – for these, discussing climate on a more abstract level may be more engaging than communication that makes climate change more immediate and visualizable. For some, encountering the tropical forest and the species in it may create a deep connection while, for others, the whole experience might be like enduring an ordeal in a hot, humid place with many insects. To engage people around climate action, we need to reach people through different ways, employing different mechanisms for communication and deliberation.

Relationality has a complexity that, ultimately, exceeds our analysis.[4] What kind of strategy for collective action is it, we might ask, to rely on something as soft and amorphous as changing people's sentiments? First of all, there is nothing soft about sentiment. Secondly, relationality is not just sentiment – connectedness can operate along the dimensions of the affective, the cognitive, and the moral, taking advantage of all of these faculties. This is why experimental work that tries to discern exactly what motivational pathway governs altruism matters only up to a certain point. In the world, people are moved to care for the other because of emotion, logic, morality (and self-love, as well). In the world, perhaps it is almost never just one thing or the other.

The success of relational strategies should vary widely depending on the specific circumstances of the intervention. For example, Sing and Swanson (2017) found other-regarding interventions to be effective in motivating climate engagement in people who already have a predisposition toward altruism. Ideology mediates the effect of strategies, as well – for example, the same study found that other-regarding framing decreased the importance of climate issues for political conservatives. It is possible that ideological frames influence how people see the other – for example, predisposing one group against seeing another group as deserving of help. As Batson suggested, altruism may require both regarding the other as deserving/valued as well as perceiving the other's need (Batson, 2011). Furthermore, ideological commitments can create a tendency among people to reject evidence that goes against tenets of the ideology, sometimes referred to as system justification (e.g., Wong-Parodi & Feygina, 2020).

7.2.4 The Social Footprint of Carbon

The relational view sees a place, society, or the world not as a field populated with independent objects, but as a web of relationships, where everyone are connected. People are connected not just with other people, but with nonhuman beings and their environments, as well. We have to be more aware of how the policies we enact affect these interconnections.

This brings us to an issue we have, thus far, not discussed, which is that policy may ignore the extent that we are all interconnected in ways invisible to the policymaker. As much has been said about the carbon

---

[4] As has been suggested, perhaps relational modes of analysis and engagement corresponds to the complexity of social-ecological systems (e.g., Cockburn et al., 2020).

footprint of society, we need to also recognize the social footprint of carbon. In its many forms, carbon is intimately connected to our lives and societies; it is part of the web of relationships that make up the social ecology of a place. The consequence of this is that decoupling from carbon will have (often unseen) effects on these intricate relationships.

How might people be motivated to wean their lifestyles away from carbon-emitting activities? The use of fossil fuels and consumption of goods dependent on carbon-emitting technologies is so tightly enmeshed into our daily lifestyles that extricating our everyday lives from carbon will entail profound shifts in these lifestyles. It may affect innumerable daily practices and maybe a radical shift in how we go about our daily round. Among the institutional remedies being proposed (and, in some places, beginning to be enacted), one is the institution of a carbon tax (see Rabe, 2018 for an introduction). The tax is meant to work in autonomous fashion, guiding individual actions through an invisible hand, transforming these actions automatically. It would require no moral commitment or individual reflection save from responding to external price signals. It need not require awareness of the consequences of one's actions or who or what might suffer from these actions. All things are hidden behind the price signal.

Consider how we might approach this from the perspective of relationality, where the objective is to not dissociate people from the other and from the consequences of their daily actions. While the price signal hides the web of relationships we are embedded in, a relational perspective strives to make these tangible. Rather than collapse our thinking into that of the consumer, the relational view strives to expand it to the steward and to encompass our place in a web of relationships.

Consider another policy instrument for carbon mitigation, that of transferable market instruments for carbon (or cap-and-trade). By instituting a carbon market, we can institute an overall cap on the total amount of carbon emitted while allowing users to trade carbon from place to place to maximize the efficiency of the resulting carbon allocations (see Hafstead, 2019 for an introduction). It is meant to be a relatively frictionless system for trading carbon and moving it from one place to another. But understanding it relationally opens us to the possibility that moving carbon from here to there will have impacts on the ways of life and the social fabric of these places. This can reveal hidden costs to both decoupling from carbon in one place and moving carbon to another. These hitherto invisible costs can be greatest on the most marginalized communities, especially in the developing world, and policymakers need to consider the social justice dimensions of climate mitigation and adaptation.

Illustrating the Social Footprint of Carbon

Southeast Los Angeles is an area comprised of small (pocket) municipalities, including Huntington Park, Bell Gardens, and others. Demographically, it is a majority-minority community, with a median income lower than the county average (IPS, 2019).

In parts of Southeast Los Angeles, many homes run small businesses literally in their front yards. One can find auto repair and engine tuning, autobody work and painting, chrome plating, engine overhaul, and other services related to the automobile industry. In short, we find communities whose commerce and lifestyles are wrapped around the internal combustion engine. As society begins to decouple from fossil fuel based transportation (and reduces the dependence on automobiles in favor of public transportation), we should think about what would happen to such neighborhoods in the transition. Would households in these areas be able to make the adjustment?

Not far from Southeast Los Angeles is the Port of Los Angeles, surrounded by the municipalities of Carson, Torrance, and others, which are the site for a number of large oil refineries. We should consider how "moving carbon" from place to place, such as with a cap-and-trade system, affect these communities. Would this allow the movement of carbon to these refineries (i.e., refineries purchasing carbon credits from elsewhere)? Would this lead to increased (relative to without cap-and-trade) or nondeclining carbon emissions in these communities? With carbon, there are other attendant pollutants, such as air toxics that are released with it, and we need to think about the environmental injustice of it (e.g., Lejano, Kan, & Chau, 2020).

Globally, we need to be more cognizant of the social footprint of carbon on developing nations and, especially, the most marginalized communities within them. The IPCC points out that many parts of the developing world will be the most vulnerable to climate change (IPCC, 2022, 14). A relational analysis should also inquire into how these same cities and communities will bear the costs of carbon mitigation and adaptation. Rough estimates from the IPCC suggest that the infrastructure costs alone will be great (Dodman et al., 2022, 6–63). Understanding places as webs of relationships begs that we consider the social costs of policy actions, as well. How will the most marginalized communities cope with the transition? Just as policies can ignore the potential of forging relationships for collective action, so too can these policies ignore their impacts on already existing webs of relationships. Relationships tend to be invisible, and often, what is essential is invisible to the eye.

It's an open question, which approach might more powerfully engender collective action and a more just climate transition. Would it be the market approach, which waves away much reflection and forethought on the part of the consumer, instituting a blanket carbon embargo through the use of a tax? Does this do away with any need to foster the cooperation of the general public? How does the blanket dictum address the differing needs and priorities of different people and places? Does it treat struggling, marginalized communities the same way as the wealthy? Or is it the relational approach, where each person takes it upon herself to respond genuinely to the needs of the environment, future generations, and the other by reorienting one's lifestyle around carbon? Which approach might lead to a more profound transformation of resource consumption in society? It is an open question, in part because one need not choose one over the other. In reality, mixed strategies abound, and it may prove to be the case with carbon mitigation.

This discussion of climate change is but a foregrounding of the potential role of relational approaches in the pursuit of individual and global action. In the rest of the book, we touch on related, key ideas that help us locate relationality in the broader conceptual landscape.

7.3 RELATIONALITY AND DIVISION

As the previous discussion on climate suggests, the relational perspective is all about encountering the other. There is another sense that such encounter can foster collective action, in that sometimes, "other" can mean that person who is ideologically diametrically opposed to ourselves, those people from the "other side." As is very clear in the case of climate, ideological division can impede progress on the issue and, when severe, can lead to policy stalemate. Part of the dynamic has to do not just with the issue at hand (and climate is only one of many collective action problems around which people are divided). An important part of the problem stems from the act of division itself, when one camp simply reacts to and rejects anything to do with the other camp. In such a situation, there is no dialogue, only diatribe.

It would seem that society is designed upon division. Any public action immediately triggers a response toward sorting self and other – left/right, liberal/collectivist, populist/elite, vax/anti-vax, and so forth. Claude Levi-Strauss wrote about the modern impulse to sort people and things in society upon classification systems (Levi-Strauss, 1966). It is the same genetic meta-narrative of sorting that is repurposed in an infinite array of situations (Lejano, 2019b). These are all variations on the theme of self alienated from other.

Is not sorting a type of relationship? Are we still seeing connections between individuals that simply flip their switches between empathy and disempathy? There are reasons to think, no, because there are categorically different types of relationship, and it is more than ties switching between bridging and dividing. In many cases, there is no real encounter with the other. Many people today cling to their respective ideological camps, listening to their respective media, staying within their secluded echo chambers (Jamieson & Cappella, 2008). The reaction to the other is not directed, fundamentally, toward a real other but its facsimile, as presented in ideologically or other socially constructed representations. Even acts of othering directed at a physical other often stem from not an encounter with the person but one's composite image of the other, filtered through a life's worth of false and preconceived biases. So, the question is: is it possible to have encounters among unfiltered, nonfalsifying selves?

There is also, possibly as damaging, the phenomenon of the so-called postmodern recession into the self. This retreat from the world outside one's self is accompanied by the loss of a sense of a larger narrative outside one's private domain. The universe shrinks into the immediately private, consumed by the lucent screen of one's cellphone. When the larger sphere of life loses its dimensionality and reverts to the concerns of the isolated ego, then maybe everything again conforms to the model of individual rationality. If we associate care with intentionality, then this a centripetal movement away from the other. People simply stop to care. There are no attachments or antagonisms with the other, and any relationship is simply a form of objectification.

To these problems, our response is to seek new ways for each to encounter the other. We do not mean the false "other," the stereotyped facsimile that people condemn on social media. On social media, people often deal only with those in their own camp within their respective echo chambers. In these media, the "other" is never actually encountered, only (falsely) represented. Discursively, the other's voice is nowhere acknowledged, their narrative often dismissed as pure untruth (Brüggemann et al., 2020). The relational turn is about finding ways that people encounter the other in authentic ways, sincerely hear their message and voice, and even engage in dialogue (Lejano & Nero, 2020).

Healing the divide may require new, imaginative strategies. The present generation has learned, too well, an othering kind of language. But there is a different way of talking and a language of inclusiveness that acknowledges the other (even the hostile other). The environmental community has to learn this language, where the other side is respected and not vilified. Media practitioners have to be cognizant of these opposed ways of talking and learn to practice a model of communication that, even when agonistic, is sincere (Habermas, 1984).

Spaces for communication across the divide have to be created. As discussed in previous chapters, collective action is fostered when local actors are able to discuss the issues among themselves and develop their own strategies, rather than having them be imposed from outside (e.g., Hourdequin, 2010). When there are spaces for genuine exchange, even ideologically opposed individuals can find some common ground (e.g., Morrissey & Boswell, 2023). These include physical spaces, as well, and there is a need to imagine cities that deliberately plan for social interactions across heterogeneous communities (e.g., Mandalaki & Fotaki, 2020). Civic spaces need to be encouraged for people to initiate joint activities, however small – those practices some called commoning, where collective actions allow shared identities to emerge (e.g., Pilny et al., 2017; Sandström, Ekman, & Lindholm, 2017). These forums might be better understood as relationships, because the world, and local communities, are facing problems (like climate change, zoonotic diseases, etc.) that are not resolved, once and for all, but require continuous civic work – in other words, new and renewed relationships. As scholars commented, in the context of local climate adaptation: "This cannot be done at a onetime meeting. It often requires continuing engagement to work through evolving proposals. Ongoing working relationships can build trust, making it easier to deal with shifting circumstances" (Susskind & Kim, 2022, 7).

7.4 RELATIONALITY AND JUSTICE

Much of this book forwards the idea that connectedness can foster collective action. Related to this, however, is the converse proposition: that disconnectedness can lead to alienation and normalizes injustice. The idea of relationality brings together otherwise distinct areas of scholarship (the commons, environmental justice).

The maldistribution of the world's goods and the unequal recognition of the rights of beings is, in a sense, a fundamental commons problem. For those with the privilege and power to change the status quo, there is nothing in their self-interest that compels them to do so. This is furthered by the alienation of self from the unjustly treated other who is objectified and not recognized as an equal being but simply an object. The turn to relationality is a response to this, for two reasons.

First, recognizing and encountering the authentic other (not the objectified other) leads us to recognize the other as equal to ourselves, deserving of resources, opportunities, and liberties just as we are. This is the foundation of an ethical response to suffering. Alienation between self and other fosters injustice because the other is regarded as a lesser being (or, in many cases, not a being at all but a category or a stereotype).

Relationality can have a further effect, when one is able to move from just principles to an ethic of care. The other is not just an equal entity, but an actual being with whom one can relate and care for. The ethic of care builds upon foundations of just principles, but it requires seeing not the categorical other but the authentic one. The relational view sees the world as a network of relationships. There are two sides to this. First, we begin to see who our potential actions might help and how. Second, we begin to inquire into who our present actions are harming.

But central to the ethic of care is seeing the other as an equal subject, not just an abstract entity but an authentic, embodied being. This means finding new means by which we can make real and tangible, the conditions faced by others who may be excluded by the mainstream – that is, victims of climate change, people of color alienated by white privilege, and nonhumans treated as simple objects of human whim.[5]

7.5 RELATIONALITY AND THE INDIVIDUAL

The modern condition is all about the subject turning its back upon the world and existing as the disattached ego. This is a turning away from the communal dimension of society, a liberation from the other. But, as the critical theorists have claimed, this liberation is also its own imprisonment (Horkheimer & Adorno, 1972). The objectification of the other is the basis of the alienation that exists between individuals and groups in

---

[5] One can understand the social movement, Black Lives Matter, as being precipitated by the use of digital media as a way of making immediate and tangible, the plight of the other, pinned down by the knee of the privileged oppressor (Lejano, Ingram, and Ingram, 2018). Another route to connectedness is making the narratives and voices of the hitherto excluded front and center of policy deliberation. An example of this is The Cassandra Project, an initiative that uses digital storytelling to highlight the voices of women fighting on the forefront of climate change mitigation and adaptation (www .environmentalcommunication.space/digitalnarratives).

society, between society and nature, and all the endless variations on the basic dichotomy between self and other.

To be sure, the relational ethic is not about denying the idea of individuality. Rather, it is about challenging a false sense of what individualism is, reducing individuality to the autonomous ego. But, as John Stuart Mill put it, individuality is "not only a coordinate element with all that is designated by the terms civilization, instruction, education, culture, but is itself a necessary part and condition of all those things" (Mill, 1859/2002, 81). In other words, individuality is part and parcel of being a relational being, contributing to the social, and advancing civilization. However, modernity reduces individuality to egoism, which is different from the way even Mill, the unabashed utilitarian, understood it. Relationality is very much about identity. Appiah puts it in these terms: "To value individuality properly just is to acknowledge the dependence of the good for each of us on relationships with others. Without these bonds, as I say, we could not come to be free selves, not least because we could not come to be selves at all" (Appiah, 2008, 20).

The modern condition is all about the subject as the individual ego. Ineluctably, an inherent part of the equation is the objectification of the other. When that other is constructed as a lesser being, in fact, simply a thing that is not a being-in-itself, a relationship of domination necessarily results. Objectification of the worker transforms the life-giving, creative act of human work into mere labor, as Hannah Arendt (1958) pointed out. Nature performs creative work, too, but modern-day relations between society and nature are such that nature is relegated to a monetizable commodity (Daly et al., 1994). Is it necessary to say that in these lie the root of the world's crises of collective action? The degradation of human creativity, especially as realized in work, has much to do with the creation of a society that seeks fulfillment mainly in the consumption of goods. Ultimately, nature is the good that is being consumed to submission. The objectification of the world's poor lies behind that complex cycle wherein poverty leads to higher population growth rates which, in turn, leads to increasing poverty (Birdsall, 1980).

Some psychologists believe that to establish a connection with another equates to enlarging one's notion of identity to encompass the other. In other words, to love the other then means to love one's self (Mayer & Frantz, 2004). In a relational framework, egoism and altruism can come together in complex, noncontradictory ways. The way forward then has to involve making who the other is tangible, making it inescapable, for all, what the other experiences, their joy, and suffering. Making the focus of society's attention the condition of the other. In other words, finding every occasion to reassert the truth that the other is equal to ourselves, and that to devalue the other is to devalue one's self.

For some, it is the particular trajectory of individualism that takes shape, especially in our times, that some refer to as a postmodern condition, that threatens collective life. That it is the decentering of the subject, its reduction to a teleology of aimless meandering from one trivial pursuit to another, that most threatens the idea of living life to the fullest. Collective action might be thought of as a grand narrative of sorts, which the postmodern temper shies away from. It certainly is true that the spirit of the blasé goes against the cultivation of an attitude of care. Rising sea levels, vaccines, media influencers, these are all signifiers unmoored from their actualities. What distinguishes news from fake news is simply an artifact of the language game being played. The inward turn to self is part of this condition, with implications of the new narcissism for collective action (e.g., Campbell et al., 2005).

What does it matter if people care? Why not just use the state's regulatory power or market incentives to make people behave in accordance with the common good? This is for the reader to reflect on. But certainly, it matters who decides what the common good is. Would it be the best thing for someone to decide what it is and to impose it on everyone – for example, how much carbon to emit? Or would it be the best for some groups to make the decision and set a carbon tax? What makes such a decision the right one for each person, and who has the right to decide, for herself, what is good? In his essay on liberty, John Stuart Mill remarks that, while it is important that the person do right things, it is just as important for her to decide what is right and to decide to do them: "He who lets the world, or his own portion of it, choose his plan of life for him, has no need for any other faculty than the ape-like one of imitation. He who chooses his plan for himself, employs all his faculties" (Mill, 1859, 55).

Engaging the individual matters strategically, as well. Think of what it takes to get states to protect wildlife and how such actions protect habitat one at a time, endangered species one at a time, and think of the vastly greater numbers of habitat and organisms (not just species, but individuals) lost that are never protected. Think of the wholesale changes in how we think and behave that are needed, and the millions of different actions needed, to be truly respectful of the nonhuman other, and the millions of small actions society does every day that threaten their habitat. It is possible that any such actions that are externally arranged and imposed on us fall short of the much greater commitment, and the uncountable number of things one has to do, to truly respect the other. Could the state or the market tell us what things must be done to be a caring parent? However long that list of sanctioned or incentivized actions, it does not equate to what it means to be a caring parent – which is not a list of things, but an entire way of being (that cannot be enumerated). Whatever is externally imposed can never be enough. To simply comply with externally imposed things would be quite different from actually caring.

There is a radical kind of reductionism that happens when good actions are prescribed by the state. First of all, it can never prescribe all that it means to be a good member of society. The reduction is carried out by the market, as well. Imagine a world where relationships between loved ones were governed by market exchange. There is a temptation to think of social capital as a form of capitalization of relationships, as if establishing of relationships were no more than banking resources for future use. To the extent that these understandings of the relational misses most of what makes relationships matter, that is the degree by which formal institutions can impede relationality.

7.6 RELATIONALITY AND SUSTAINABILITY

The relational dimension is often missing from discussions of sustainability and resilience. These latter two concepts are, most often, associated with system states (and the degree that they maintain over time or recover after a perturbation). There is something fundamentally objectivist with these system concepts and their descriptions of systems of objects and their functioning. However, underlying sustainability and resilience are processes that govern how objects function, and these are related to the relationships that enmesh them. A system with elements that are interconnected and mutually supportive can function coherently, sustainably, and resiliently. Systems with missing or perverse relationships can operate in destructive fashion. The sustainability or resilience of the system is something that emerges from the working out of relationships among its elements (Lejano, 2019a). Sustainability and resilience are states that emerge from the degree and kinds of connectedness found in a system. These connections especially pertain to those between humans and non-humans. In contrast, coupled systems approaches, while essential, can tend towards a substantialism that keeps humans and nature separate (West et al., 2020).

For example, when administrative systems and market processes operating in isolation from their ecological base, then we find systems that continually degrade the latter (Daly, 1993). When consumers in the industrialized nations are blind to the living conditions of those in poor enclaves in the developing world, perverse patterns of consumption are more readily accepted as the status quo.

Relationality can be thought of as a condition that can be studied on its own, apart from the concepts of sustainability or resilience, but perhaps more fruitfully as necessary aspects of them (Lejano, 2019a; Walsh, Böhme, & Wamsler, 2021). There is a need to more closely examine the role of connectedness and disconnectedness and to study patterns and functionings of relationships that underpin conditions of sustainability and resilience. Relationality can further transform commons research to encompass more than managing a socio-ecological system, seeing it not just as a system but as the constitution of community – a notion sometimes referred to as commoning (e.g., Nieto-Romero, 2019; Nayak & Berkes, 2022). In her writings on commoning and the commons, Federici invokes a notion of community "not as a not as a gated reality, a grouping of people joined by exclusive interests separating them from others… but rather as a quality of relations, a principle of cooperation, and a responsibility to each other and to the earth, the forests, the seas, the animals" (Federici, 2011, 386).

The notion of community is becoming more expansive, especially in this digital age. Correspondingly, we need to take advantage of digital media in building a sense of connectedness. Many of the most pressing problems of our times have to do with global crises (i.e., climate change, the pandemic), and people need to develop an expansive ethic that responds to these needs. Digital media may offer new ways to connect. Stokols, writing about the psychology of the Anthropocene, suggests: "wide-ranging mental maps of virtually experienced environments may enable people to identify and share commonality with those distant places as well as with their more immediate local surroundings… to develop a global rather than an exclusively local or national place identity – and accordingly, act in ways that protect regional and global ecosystems as well as their more immediate local surroundings" (Stokols, 2020, 25).

To be clear, what we are talking about is not about lapsing into a postmodern angst where one is paralyzed in the face of local and global crises that seem to leave one powerless. Rather, we mean living a life rooted in community with others, responding to them with an ethic of care.

7.7 CLOSING THOUGHTS

A common truism about collective action problems says that we must find ways to channel people's self-interest so that self-interested individuals act for the common good. The standard assumption is that one can *always* rely on people to act out of self-interest. The same conventional wisdom posits that solving these problems through enlightened altruism cannot work because we can *never* rely on people's altruism. These notions, however commonsensical, are based on a silhouette of the human person. Conversely, why is it that we can rely on people to act to protect their family, their friends, and other loved ones? In the countless prisoner's dilemma situations of life that one encounters involving these loved ones, why is it, to no one's surprise, that altruism and collective action almost always result? The answer must be that we are not simply atoms in a void. And part of the tragedy is that, too often, we assume we are and design our institutions correspondingly. As we have discussed in previous chapters, people are not self-serving utilitarian automatons. As importantly, neither are they rule-bound collectivist ones. We need to take into account that the person is both the individual self and the connected one.

For scholars, these considerations suggest multiple directions for future work. The most fundamental task is to probe more deeply into the role of connectedness in fostering altruism in the individual and collective action in the group. Can refinements in the design of experimental games and social psychological research better discern the action of empathy from related mechanisms (such as warm-glow altruism) that promote other-regarding behavior? What role do other-regard and empathy play in the dynamics of social networks?

There are equally promising avenues for research on institutional design. Are there policies and institutions for collective action that can be designed chiefly around relationality? How do relational mechanisms complement conventional policy instruments such as state regulations and market instruments? Can we reexamine the rich constellation of institutions studied by Ostrom and colleagues and see them through a relational lens? Can we, more systematically, analyze the relational effects of policies?

We should more deeply investigate how relationality is at work in the world, moving people to act in pro-social and pro-environmental ways. There are countless examples of programs and initiatives that implicitly build on the relational in order to promote their causes. How might we further tap into this potential? The most important steps forward are for practitioners, who should learn to tap into the power of connectedness.

The strategy is not simply to urge people to consider others and be altruistic – have we not been doing this since time immemorial? It is to create mechanisms, institutions, pedagogies, that make the other visible, to foreground the experiences, sufferings, joys, and circumstances of others and make them tangible, and to connect. There are too many things that are too invisible for us to care about, like schoolchildren dealing with glacial melt flooding their town, or smallholder coffee farmers in Brazil losing crops to frost, or animals displaced by brushfires in the outback. We need to channel our creativity to bring all these to light, to encounter, look into the eyes of the other and realize, we are not so separate.

In the end, what saves the world may be found in the space in between each of us, in the life that emerges in this space. We can translate it into a concept like relational capital but, ultimately, the idea of a good never does measure up. If it is a kind of good at all, it is only of value when you find it in the other. We are more than atoms. Relationality defines us, which we realize within the most common of experiences, as we grasp the hermeneutic of self-and-other, when we reach out to the other only to find ourselves, and realize, just how much we are all creatures of affinity.

References

Agrawal, A., & Goyal, S. (2001). Group size and collective action: Third party monitoring in common pool resources. *Comparative Political Studies*, 34(1), 63–93.

Agrawal, A., & Ostrom, E. (2001). Collective action, property rights, and decentralization in resource use in India and Nepal. *Politics & Society*, 29(4), 485–514.

Agarwal, A., Narain, S., & Sharma, A. (2017). The global commons and environmental justice – climate change. In Thompson, P. (Ed.), *Environmental Justice* (pp. 171–199). Routledge, New York.

Aksoy, B., & Palma, M. A. (2019). The effects of scarcity on cheating and in-group favoritism. *Journal of Economic Behavior & Organization*, 165, 100–117.

Alcock, J. (1993). Exadaptations. *Behavioral and Brain Sciences*, 16(2), 283–284.

Althor, G., Watson, J. E., & Fuller, R. A. (2016). Global mismatch between greenhouse gas emissions and the burden of climate change. *Scientific Reports*, 6(1), 20281–20286.

Altman, I., & Low, S. (1992). *Place Attachment. Human Behavior and Environment*, 1st Edition. Springer, New York.

Amiot, C. E., & Bastian, B. (2015). Toward a psychology of human-animal relations. *Psychological Bulletin*, 141(1), 6–47.

Anderies, J. M., & Janssen, M. A. (2013). Robustness of social? ecological systems: Implications for public policy. *Policy Studies Journal*, 41(3), 513–536.

Anderies, J. M., Janssen, M. A., Bousquet, F., Cardenas, J. C., Castillo, D., Lopez, M. C., ... & Wutich, A. (2011). The challenge of understanding decisions in experimental studies of common pool resource governance. *Ecological Economics*, 70(9), 1571–1579.

Anderson, B., & McFarlane, C. (2011). Assemblage and geography. *Area*, 43(2), 124–127.

Andersson, K. (2006). Understanding decentralized forest governance: An application of the institutional analysis and development framework. *Sustainability: Science, Practice and Policy*, 2(1), 25–35.

Andersson, K. P., & Ostrom, E. (2008). Analyzing decentralized resource regimes from a polycentric perspective. *Policy Sciences*, 41(1), 71–93.

Andersson, K. P., Chang, K., & Molina-Garzón, A. (2020). Voluntary leadership and the emergence of institutions for self-governance. *Proceedings of the National Academy of Sciences*, 117(44), 27292–27299.

Andreoni, J. (1990). Impure altruism and donations to public goods: A theory of warm-glow giving. *The Economic Journal*, 100(401), 464–477.

Andreoni, J., & Vesterlund, L. (1997). *Which is the Fair Sex? Gender Differences in Altruism*. University of Wisconsin, Madison, Mimeo.

Appiah, A. (2008). *Experiments in Ethics*. Harvard University Press, Cambridge, Mass.

Araral, E. (2014). Ostrom, hardin and the commons: A critical appreciation and a revisionist view. *Environmental Science & Policy*, 36, 11–23.

Arendt, H. (1958). *The Human Condition*, University of Chicago Press, Chicago.

Aron, A., Aron, E. N., & Smollan, D. (1992). Inclusion of other in the self scale and the structure of interpersonal closeness. *Journal of Personality and Social Psychology*, 63, 596–612.

Athanases, S. Z., & Sanchez, S. L. (2020). "A Caesar for our time": Toward empathy and perspective-taking in new teachers' drama practices in diverse classrooms. *Research in Drama Education: The Journal of Applied Theatre and Performance*, 25(2), 236–255.

Aumann, R., & Shapley, L. (1976). Long-term competition: A game-theoretic analysis. Mimeo, Hebrew University. Reprinted in: Megiddo, N. (Ed.), 1994. *Essays in Game Theory in Honor of Michael Maschler* (pp. 1–15). Springer-Verlag, Berlin.

Bain, P. G., Hornsey, M. J., Bongiorno, R., & Jeffries, C. (2012). Promoting pro-environmental action in climate change deniers. *Nature Climate Change*, 2(8), 600–603.

Bal, P. M., & Veltkamp, M. (2013). How does fiction reading influence empathy? An experimental investigation on the role of emotional transportation. *PLoS One*, 8(1), e55341.

Baland, J.-M., & Platteau, J.-P. (1996). *Halting Degradation of Natural Resources: Is There a Role for Rural Communities?* Clarendon Press, Oxford.

Barazza, J. A., & Zak, P. J. (2013). Chapter 18. Oxytocin instantiates empathy and produces prosocial behaviours. In Choleris, E., Pfaff, D. W., & M. Kavaliers (Eds.), *Oxytocin, Vasopressin and Related Peptides in the Regulation of Behaviour* (pp. 331–342). Cambridge University Press, Cambridge.

Barclay, P. (2012). Harnessing the power of reputation: Strengths and limits for promoting cooperative behaviors. *Evolutionary Psychology*, 10(5), 147470491201000509.

Barclay, P., & van Vugt, M. (2015). The evolutionary psychology of human prosociality: Adaptations, byproducts, and mistakes. In D. A. Schroeder, & W. G. Graziano (Eds.), *The Oxford Handbook of Prosocial Behavior* (pp. 37–60). Oxford University Press, Oxford.

Barraza, J., & Zak, P. (2009). Empathy toward strangers triggers oxytocin release and subsequent generosity. *New York Academy of Sciences*, 1167(1), 182–189.

Bartels, K., & Turnbull, N. (2019). Relational public administration: A synthesis and heuristic classification of relational approaches. *Public Management Review*, 1–23.

Batavia, C., Bruskotter, J. T., Jones, J. A., Vucetich, J. A., Gosnell, H., & Nelson, M. P. (2018). Nature for whom? How type of beneficiary influences the effectiveness of conservation outreach messages. *Biological Conservation*, 228, 158–166.

Batson, C. D. (1987). Prosocial motivation: Is it ever truly altruistic? In L. Berkowitz (Ed.), *Advances in Experimental Social Psychology* (Vol. 20, pp. 65–122). New York: Academic.

Batson, C. D. (Ed.), (2011). *Altruism in Humans* (p. 329). Oxford University Press, Oxford.

Batson, C. D., & Moran, T. (1999). Empathy-induced altruism in a prisoner's dilemma. *European Journal of Social Psychology*, 29(7), 909–924.

Batson, C. D., & Shaw, L. L. (1991). Evidence for altruism: Toward a pluralism of prosocial motives. *Psychological Inquiry*, 2(2), 107–122.

Batson, C. D., Ahmad, N., Lishner, D. A., Tsang, J., Snyder, C. R., & Lopez, S. J. (2002). Chapter 35. Empathy and altruism. In Snyder, C. R., & S. J. Lopez (Eds.), *Handbook of Positive Psychology* (pp. 161–174). Oxford University Press, Oxford.

Batson, C. D., Chang, J., Orr, R., & Rowland, J. (2002). Empathy, attitudes, and action: Can feeling for a member of a stigmatized group motivate one to help the group? *Personality and Social Psychology Bulletin*, 28(12), 1656–1666.

Batson, C. D., Duncan, B. D., Ackerman, P., Buckley, T., & Birch, K. (1981). Is empathic emotion a source of altruistic motivation? *Journal of Personality and Social Psychology*, 40(2), 290.

Batson, C. D. et al., (2002). "Empathy, attitudes, and action: Can feeling for a member of a stigmatized group motivate one to help the group?" *Personality and Social Psychology Bulletin*, 28(12), 1656–1666., doi:10.1177/014616702237647.

Batson, C. D., Pate, S., Lawless, H., Sparkman, P., Lambers, S., & Worman, B. (1979). Helping under conditions of common threat: Increased "we-feeling" or ensuring reciprocity. *Social Psychology Quarterly*, 42(4), 410–414.

Baumol, W. J., & Oates, W. E. (1988). *The Theory of Environmental Policy*, 2nd Ed., Cambridge University Press, Cambridge and New York.

Benford, R. D., & Snow, D. A. (2000). Framing processes and social movements: An overview and assessment. *Annual Review of Sociology*, 26(1), 611–639.

Benhabib, S. (1987). General and concrete others. In S. Benhabib, & D. Cornell (Eds.), *Feminism as Critique* (pp. 77–96). Polity Press, Cambridge.

Benhabib, S. (1992). *Situating the Self: Gender, Community, and Postmodernism in Contemporary Ethics*. Routledge, New York.

Benjamin, P., Lam, W. F., Ostrom, E., & Shivakoti, G. (1994). *Institutions, Incentives and Irrigation in Nepal*. Indiana University, Bloomington, IN.

Bennett, R. (2003). Factors underlying the inclination to donate to particular types of charity. *International Journal of Nonprofit and Voluntary Sector Marketing*, 8(1), 12–29.

Berchin, I. I., Valduga, I. B., Garcia, J., & de Andrade, J. B. S. O. (2017). Climate change and forced migrations: An effort towards recognizing climate refugees. *Geoforum*, 84, 147–150.

Berenguer, J. (2007). "The effect of empathy in proenvironmental attitudes and behaviors." *Environment & Behavior*, 39(2):269–283.

Berkes, F. (2002). Cross-scale institutional linkages: Perspectives from the bottom up. In Ostrom, E., Dietz, T., Dolsak, N., Stern, P. C., Stonich, S., & E. U. Weber (Eds.), *The Drama of the Commons* (pp. 293–321). National Academies Press, Washington, D.C.

Berkes, F. (2017). *Sacred Ecology*. Routledge, New York.

Berkes, F., Colding, J., & Folke, C. (2000). Rediscovery of traditional ecological knowledge as adaptive management. *Ecological Applications*, 10(5), 1251–1262.

Bern, C. et al. (1993). Risk factors for mortality in the Bangladesh cyclone of 1991. *Bull World Health Organ*, 71(1), 73.

Bertin, P., Nera, K., Hamer, K., Uhl-Haedicke, I., & Delouvée, S. (2021). Stand out of my sunlight: The mediating role of climate change conspiracy beliefs in the relationship between national collective narcissism and acceptance of climate science. *Group Processes & Intergroup Relations*, 24(5), 738–758.

Bevir, M., & Rhodes, R. A. W. (2022). All you need is... a network: The rise of interpretive public administration. *Public Administration*, 100(1),149–160.

Biermann, F., & Möller, I. (2019). Rich man's solution? climate engineering discourses and the marginalization of the Global South. *International Environmental Agreements: Politics, Law and Economics*, 19(2), 151–167.

Billen, G., Garnier, J., & Barles, S. (2012). History of the urban environmental imprint: Introduction to a multidisciplinary approach to the long-term relationships between Western cities and their hinterland.

Binngiesser, J., Wilhelm, C., & Randler, C. (2013). Attitudes towards animals among German children and adolescents. *Anthrozoös*, 26, 325–339.

Birdsall, N. (1980). Population growth and poverty in the developing world. *Population Bulletin*, 35(5), 1–48.

Bodin, Ö., & Crona, B. I. (2009). The role of social networks in natural resource governance: What relational patterns make a difference? *Global Environmental Change*, 19(3), 366–374.

Bohnet, I., & Frey, B. S. (1999). Social distance and other-regarding behavior in dictator games: Comment. *American Economic Review*, 89(1), 335–339.

Bolderdijk, J. W., Steg, L., Geller, E. S., Lehman, P. K., & Postmes, T. (2013). Comparing the effectiveness of monetary versus moral motives in environmental campaigning. *Nature Climate Change*, 3, 413–416. doi: 10.1038/nclimate1767

Bolton, G., & Katok, E. (1995). An experimental test for gender differences in beneficent behavior. *Economics Letters*, 48(3–4), 287–92.

Bolton, G. E., & Ockenfels, A. (2000). ERC: A theory of equity, reciprocity, and competition. *American Economic Review*, 90(1), 166–193.

Bouckaert, G. (2012). Trust and public administration. *Administration*, 60(1), 91–115.

Bourdieu, P., & Wacquant, L. (1992). *An Invitation to Reflexive Sociology*. The University of Chicago Press, Chicago and London.

Bourdieu, P. (1977). *Outline of a Theory of Practice* (translated by R. Nice). Cambridge University Press, Cambridge.

Boy, J., Pandey, A. V., Emerson, J., Satterthwaite, M., Nov, O., & Bertini, E. (2017). Showing people behind data: Does anthropomorphizing visualizations elicit more empathy for human rights data? In Proceedings of the 2017 CHI Conference on Human Factors in Computing Systems (pp. 5462–5474).

Boyd, R., & Richerson, P. J. (2002). Group beneficial norms can spread rapidly in a structured population. *Journal of Theoretical Biology*, 215(3), 287–296.

Bredicean, C., Tamasan, S. C., Lungeanu, D., Giurgi-Oncu, C., Stoica, I. P., Panfil, A. L., ... & Patrascu, R. (2021). Burnout toll on empathy would mediate the missing professional support in the COVID-19 outbreak. *Risk Management and Healthcare Policy*, 14, 2231.

Broome, J. (2008). The ethics of climate change. *Scientific American*, 298(6), 96–102.

Brüggemann, M., Elgesem, D., Bienzeisler, N., Gertz, H. D., & Walter, S. (2020). Mutual group polarization in the blogosphere: Tracking the hoax discourse on climate change. *International Journal of Communication*, 14, 24.

Brügger, A. (2020). Understanding the psychological distance of climate change: The limitations of construal level theory and suggestions for alternative theoretical perspectives. *Global Environmental Change*, 60, 102023.

Brügger, A., Morton, T. A., & Dessai, S. (2016). "Proximising" climate change reconsidered: A construal level theory perspective. *Journal of Environmental Psychology*, 46, 125–142.

Brugnach, M., De Waard, S., Dubois, D., & Farolfi, S. (2021). Relational quality and uncertainty in common pool water management: An exploratory lab experiment. *Scientific Reports*, 11(1), 1–14.

Bruner, J. (1987). Life as Narrative. *Social Research*, 54(1), 11–32.

Bruner, J. (2003). The narrative construction of reality. In M. Mateas, & P. Sengers (Eds.), *Narrative Intelligence* (pp. 41–62). John Benjamins, Amsterdam.

Buber, M. (1937). *I and Thou*, transl. by Ronald Gregor Smith, Edinburgh: T. and T. Scribners, New York. Originally published in.

Burt, C. D., & Strongman, K. (2005). Use of images in charity advertising: Improving donations and compliance rates. *International Journal of Organisational Behaviour*, 8(8), 571–580.

Burt, R. S. (2000). The network structure of social capital. *Research in Organizational Behavior* 22, 345–423. Greenwich, CT: JAI Press.

CAF, Charities Aid Foundation (2021). CAF World Giving Index 2021, Charities Aid Foundation, London. www.cafonline.org/docs/default-source/about-us-research/cafworldgivingindex2021_report_web2_100621.pdf

Camerer, C. F., & Thaler, R. H. (1995). Anomalies: Ultimatums, dictators and manners. *Journal of Economic Perspectives*, 9(2), 209–219.

Campbell, W. K., Bush, C. P., Brunell, A. B., & Shelton, J. (2005). Understanding the social costs of narcissism: The case of the tragedy of the commons. *Personality and Social Psychology Bulletin*, 31(10), 1358–1368.

Čapek, S. M. (2010). Foregrounding nature: An invitation to think about shifting nature–city boundaries. *City & Community*, 9(2), 208–224.

Capstick, S., Lorenzoni, I., Corner, A., & Whitmarsh, L. (2014). Prospects for radical emissions reduction through behavior and lifestyle change. *Carbon Management*, 5(4), 429–445.

Carlsson, L., & Sandström, A. (2008). Network governance of the commons. *International Journal of the Commons*, 2(1), 33–54.

Carré, A., Stefaniak, N., D'Ambrosio, F., Bensalah, L., & Besche-Richard, C. (2013). The basic empathy scale in adults (BES-A): Factor structure of a revised form. *Psychological Assessment*, 25(3), 679–691. doi:10.1037/a0003229

Chan, A. A. H. (2012). Anthropomorphism as a conservation tool. *Biodiversity and Conservation*, 21(7), 1889–1892.

Chu, H., & Yang, J. Z. (2018). Taking climate change here and now–mitigating ideological polarization with psychological distance. *Global Environmental Change*, 53, 174–181.

Cialdini R. B., Darby B. K., & Vincent J. E. (1973a). Transgression and altruism: A case for hedonism. *Journal of Experimental Social Psychology* 70, 666–677.

Cialdini R. B., Darby B. K., & Vincent J. E. (1973b). Transgression and altruism: A case for hedonism. *Journal of Experimental Social Psychology* 9(6), 502–516.

Cochard, F., Le Gallo, J., Georgantzis, N., & Tisserand, J. C. (2021). Social preferences across different populations: Meta-analyses on the ultimatum game and dictator game. *Journal of Behavioral and Experimental Economics*, 90(February), 101613.

Cockburn, J., Rosenberg, E., Copteros, A., Cornelius, S. F. A., Libala, N., Metcalfe, L., & van der Waal, B. (2020). A relational approach to landscape stewardship: Towards a new perspective for multi-actor collaboration. *Land*, 9(7), 224.

Coleman, E. A., & Steed, B. C. (2009). Monitoring and sanctioning in the commons: An application to forestry. *Ecological Economics*, 68(7), 2106–2113.

Comte, A. (1851). *Système de politique positive*. Carilian-Goeury, Paris.

Constantino, S. M., & Weber, E. U. (2021). Decision-making under the deep uncertainty of climate change: The psychological and political agency of narratives. *Current Opinion in Psychology*, 42, 151–159.

Cooke, G., & Muir, R. (Eds.), (2012). *The Relational State: How Recognising the Importance of Human Relation-Ships Could Revolutionise the Role of the State*. Institute for Public Policy Research, London.

Cox, M., Villamayor-Tomas, S., Ban, N. C., Epstein, G., Evans, L., Fleischman, F., ... & Schoon, M. (2020). From concepts to comparisons: A resource for diagnosis and measurement in social-ecological systems. *Environmental Science & Policy*, 107, 211–216.

Crona, B. I. (2006). Supporting and enhancing development of heterogeneous ecological knowledge among resource users in a Kenyan Seascape. *Ecology & Society* 11, 32.

Cunningham, R., Cvitanovic, C., Measham, T., Jacobs, B., Dowd, A. M., & Harman, B. (2016). Engaging communities in climate adaptation: The potential of social networks. *Climate Policy*, 16(7), 894–908.

Curran, B. J., Jenkins, M. A., & Tedeschi, P. (2019). Chapter 14: The global and cross-cultural reach of trauma-informed animal-assisted interventions. In Tedeschi, P., & M. A. Jenkins (Eds.), *Transforming Trauma: Resilience and Healing through Our Connections with Animals* (pp. 423–462). Purdue University Press, Lafayette, Indiana.

Curto-Millet, D., & Corsín Jiménez, A. (2022). The sustainability of open source commons. *European Journal of Information Systems*, 1–19. DOI:10.1080/0960085X.2022.2046516.

Czap, N. V., Czap, H. J., Banerjee, S., & Burbach, M. E. (2019). Encouraging farmers' participation in the conservation stewardship program: A field experiment. *Ecological Economics*, 161(July), 130–143.

Czap, N., Czap, H., Lynne, G., & M. Burbach (2015). Walk in my shoes: Nudging for empathy conservation. *Ecological Economics*, 118, 147–158.

Daly, H. E. (1984). Alternative strategies for integrating economics and ecology. In Jansson, A.-M. (Ed.), *Integration of Economy and Ecology: An Outlook for the Eighties* (pp. 19–29). University of Stockholm, Stockholm, Sweden.

Daly, H. E., Cobb Jr, J. B., & Cobb, J. B. (1994). *For the Common Good: Redirecting the Economy Toward Community, The Environment, and a Sustainable Future (No. 73)*. Beacon Press.

Daly, H. (1993). Steady-state economics: A new paradigm. *New Literary History* 24(4), 811–816.

Darian, J. C., Tucci, L., Newman, C. M., & Naylor, L. (2015). An analysis of consumer motivations for purchasing fair trade coffee. *Journal of International Consumer Marketing*, 27(4), 318–327.

Davis, J. E. (Ed.), (2012). *Stories of Change: Narrative and Social Movements*. SUNY Press, Albany, NY.

Davis, M. H. (2015). Empathy and prosocial behavior. In D. A. Schroeder, & W. G. Graziano (Eds.), *Oxford Library of Psychology* (pp. 282–306). The Oxford handbook of prosocial behavior. Oxford University Press, Oxford.

Dawes, C. T., Loewen, P. J., & Fowler, J. H. (2011). Social preferences and political participation. *The Journal of Politics*, 73(3), 845–856.

Dawes, R. M., & R. H. Thaler (1988). Anomalies: Cooperation. *Journal of Economic Perspectives*, 2(3), 187–197.

De Moor, T., & Tukker, A. (2015). Survival without sanctioning: The relationship between institutional resilience and methods of dealing with free-riding on early modern Dutch commons. *Jahrbuch für Geschichte des ländlichen Raumes*, 12(2015), 175–206.

De Moor, T., Farjam, M., Van Weeren, R., Bravo, G., Forsman, A., Ghorbani, A., & Dehkordi, M. A. E. (2021). Taking sanctioning seriously: The impact of sanctions on the resilience of historical commons in Europe. *Journal of Rural Studies*, 87, 181–188.

De Moor, T., Laborda-Pemán, M., Lana-Berasain, J. M., Van Weeren, R., & Winchester, A. (2016). Ruling the commons. Introducing a new methodology for the analysis of historical commons. *International Journal of the Commons*, 10(2), 529–588.

de Waal, F. B. M. (2008). Putting the altruism back into altruism: The evolution of empathy. *Annual Review of Psychology*, 59, 279–300. doi:10.1146/annurev.psych.59.103006.093625

Decety, J. (2011). Neuroscience of empathic responding. In Stephanie, L., & Brown, R. (Eds.), *Moving Beyond Self-Interest: Perspectives from Evolutionary Biology, Neuroscience, and the Social Sciences*, Oxford University Press, Oxford.

Decety, J., & Grèzes, J. (2006). The power of simulation: Imagining one's own and other's behavior. *Brain Research*, 1079(1), 4–14.

Deci, E. L., & Ryan, R. M. (1985). *Intrinsic Motivation and Self-Determination in Human Behavior*. Plenum Press, New York.

Deer, L., Fire, J.,& Erdoes, R. (1972). *Lame Deer, Seeker of Visions, Life of a Sioux Medicine Man*. Simon & Schuster, New York.

Deleuze, G., & Guattari, F. (1987). *A Thousand Plateaus: Capitalism and Schizophrenia* (B. Massumi, Trans.). University of Minnesota Press, London.

DeWall, C. N., & Baumeister, R. F. (2006). Alone but feeling no pain: Effects of social exclusion on physical pain tolerance and pain threshold, affective forecasting, and interpersonal empathy. *Journal of Personality and Social Psychology*, 91(1), 1–15.

Dierwechter, Y., & Taufen Wessells, A. (2013). The uneven localisation of climate action in metropolitan Seattle. *Urban Studies*, 50(7), 1368–1385.

Dietz, T. (2015). Altruism, self-interest, and energy consumption. *Proceedings of the National Academy of Sciences of the United States of America*, 112, 1654–1655. doi: 10.1073/pnas.1423686112

Dietz, T., & Henry, A. D. (2008). Context and the commons. *Proceedings of the National Academy of Sciences*, 105(36), 13189–13190.

Dietz, T., Ostrom, E., & Stern, P. C. (2003). The struggle to govern the commons. *Science*, 302(5652), 1907–1912.

Dillahunt, T., Becker, G., Mankoff, J., & Kraut, R. (2008, May). Motivating environmentally sustainable behavior changes with a virtual polar bear. In Pervasive 2008 Workshop Proceedings (Vol. 8, pp. 58–62). Workshop held at the 6th International Conference on Pervasive Computing, May 19th, 2008, Sydney, Australia.

Dodge, J., Ospina, S. M., & Foldy, E. G. (2005). Integrating rigor and relevance in public administrationscholarship: The contribution of narrative inquiry. *Public Administration Review,* 65(3), 286–300.

Dodge, J., Saz-Carranza, A., & Ospina, S. M. (2019). Narrative inquiry in public network research. In Joris V. J., Keast, R., & Koliba C. (Eds.), *Networks and Collaboration in the Public Sector* (pp. 82–106). Routledge, London.

Dodman, D., Hayward, B., Pelling, M., Castan, B. V., Chow, W., Chu, E., ... & Ziervogel, G. (2022). Chapter 6: Cities, settlements and key infrastructure. In H.-O. Pörtner et al. (Eds.), *Climate Change 2022: Impacts, Adaptation, and Vulnerability*. Contribution of Working Group II to the Sixth Assessment Report of the Intergovernmental Panel on Climate Change. Cambridge University Press, Cambridge.

Domantay, J. (1953). The turtle fisheries in turtle islands. *Bull. Fish. Soc. Philippines*, 3–4, 3–27.

Domes, G., Heinrichs, M., Michel, A., Berger, C., & Herpertz, S. C. (2007). Oxytocin improves 'Mind-Reading' in humans. *Biological Psychiatry*, 61(6), 731–733.

Dr Dog (2021). AnimalsAsia webpage at www.animalsasia.org/hk-en/our-work/cat-and-dog-welfare/what-we-do/dr-dog.html. Accessed June 30, 2021.

Druckman, J. N., Klar, S., Krupnikov, Y., Levendusky, M., & Ryan, J. B. (2022). (Mis) estimating affective polarization. *The Journal of Politics*, 84(2), 1106–1117.

Dubois, G., Sovacool, B., Aall, C., Nilsson, M., Barbier, C., Herrmann, A., ... & Sauerborn, R. (2019). It starts at home? Climate policies targeting household consumption and behavioral decisions are key to low-carbon futures. *Energy Research & Social Science*, 52, 144–158.

Durkheim, E. (1893). (1964). *The Division of Labor in Society* (G. Simpson, Trans.). Free Press, New York.

Eckel, C., & P. Grossman (1998). Are women less selfish than men: Evidence from dictator experiments. *Economic Journal*, May 1998a, 108(448), 726–735.

Eckerman, I. (2005). *The Bhopal Saga–Causes and Consequences of the World's Largest Industrial Disaster*. Universities Press, Hyderabad, India. doi:10.13140/2.1.3457.5364. ISBN 978-81-7371-515-0.

Eklund, J., Andersson- Straberg, T., & Hansen, E. M. (2009). "I've also experienced loss and fear": Effects of prior similar experience on empathy. *Scandinavian Journal of Psychology*, 50(1), 65–69.

Empatico (2019). Empatico 2018–2019 Evaluation Study. Working paper, unpublished manuscript at https://drive.google.com/file/d/1GUh8FSgP25TWY 2YJED4Kn5pNaiTPamQn/view?pli=1. Accessed June 1, 2022.

Enfield, N. J., & Levinson, S. C. (2006). *Roots of Human Sociality*. Berg, New York.

Ernstson, H., So¨ rlin, S., & Elmqvist, T. (2009). Social movements and ecosystem services- the role of social network structure in protecting and managing urban green areas in stockholm. *Ecology & Society*, 13, 39.

Falk, A., Fehr, E., & Fischbacher, U. (2002). Appropriating the Commons: A Theoretical Explanation. In E. Ostrom, et al. (Eds.), *The Drama of the Commons*. National Academy Press, Washington, D.C.

Federici, S. (2011). Feminism and the Politics of the Commons. www.bakonline .org/wp-content/uploads/2020/04/FEDERICI_Feminism-and-the-Politics-of-the-Commons_FORMER-WEST-2016.pdf. Accessed May 1, 2022.

Fehr, E., & Schmidt, K. M. (2006). Chapter 8. The economics of fairness, reciprocity and altruism–experimental evidence and new theories. In Kolm, S-C., & Ythier, J. M. (Eds.), *Handbook of the Economics of Giving, Altruism and Reciprocity* (pp. 615–691). North-Holland, Amsterdam.

Feinberg, A., Hooijschuur, E., Rogge, N., Ghorbani, A., & Herder, P. (2021). Sustaining collective action in urban community gardens. *Journal of Artificial Societies and Social Simulation*, 24(3), 3. DOI: 10.18564/jasss.4506

Ferraro, P. J., & Price, M. K. (2013). Using nonpecuniary strategies to influence behavior: Evidence from a large-scale field experiment. *Review of Economics and Statistics*, 95(1), 64–73.

Ferraro, P. J., Miranda, J. J., & Price, M. K. (2011). The persistence of treatment effects with norm-based policy instruments: Evidence from a randomized environmental policy experiment. *American Economic Review*, 101(3), 318–322. www.doi.org/10.1257/aer.101.3.318.

Fischer, C. (2014). "Slumming It." In Blog: Made in America. Boston Review. http://bostonreview.net/blog/claude-fischer-made-america-alice-goffman-slum-ethnography. Accessed June 14, 2021.

Fisher, R., Ury, W. L., & Patton, B. (2011). *Getting to Yes: Negotiating Agreement Without Giving In*. Penguin, New York.

Fiske, S. T. (2009). From dehumanization and objectification, to rehumanization: Neuroimaging studies on the building blocks of empathy. *Annals of the New York Academy of Sciences*, 1167, 31.

Flood, M., Dresher, M., Tucker, A., & Device, F. (1950). Prisoner's dilemma: Game theory. *Experimental Economics* (p. 54). Rand Corporation, Santa Monica, California.

Foucault, M. (1980). *Power/knowledge: Selected Interviews and Other Writings, 1972–1977.* Vintage, New York.

Friedman, D., & McAdam, D. (1992). Collective identities and activism: networks, choices, and the life of a social movement. In Morris, A. D., & Mueller, C. (Eds.), *Frontiers of Social Movement Theory* (pp. 156–173). Yale University Press, New Haven, CT.

Frischmann, B. M., Madison, M. J., & Strandburg, K. J. (Eds.), (2014). *Governing Knowledge Commons.* Oxford University Press.

Fultz, J., Batson, C. D., Fortenbach, V. A., McCarthy, P. M., & Varney, L. L. (1986). Social evaluation and the empathy-altruism hypothesis. *Journal of Personality and Social Psychology,* 50(4), 761–769.

Furnham, A. (1995). The just world, charitable giving and attitudes to disability. *Personal and Individual Differences,* 19, 577–583.

Gabriel, Y. (2010). Beyond scripts and rules: Emotion, fantasy and care in contemporary service work. In *Emotionalizing Organizations and Organizing Emotions* (pp. 42–62). Palgrave Macmillan, London.

Galinsky, A. D., Maddux, W. W., Gilin, D., & White, J. B. (2008). Why it pays to get inside the head of your opponent: The differential effects of perspective taking and empathy in negotiations. *Psychological Science,* 19(4), 378–384.

Garner, B. (2017). Communicating social support during crises at the farmers' market: A social exchange approach to understanding customer?farmer communal relationships. *International Journal of Consumer Studies,* 41(4), 422–430.

Gatiso, T. T., Vollan, B., & Nuppenau, E. A. (2015). Resource scarcity and democratic elections in commons dilemmas: An experiment on forest use in Ethiopia. *Ecological Economics,* 114, 199–207.

Geiger, N., Swim, J. K., & Glenna, L. (2019). Spread the green word: A social community perspective into environmentally sustainable behavior. *Environment and Behavior,* 51(5), 561–589.

Genevsky, A., Västfjäll, D., Slovic, P., & Knutson, B. (2013). Neural underpinnings of the identifiable victim effect: Affect shifts preferences for giving. *Journal of Neuroscience,* 33(43), 17188–17196.

Gerlak, A. K., & Heikkila, T. (2007). Collaboration and institutional endurance in US water policy. *PS: Political Science & Politics,* 40(1), 55–60.

Gibson, C., Williams, J., & Ostrom, E. (2005). Local enforcement and better forests. *World Development,* 33(2), 273–284.

Giest, S., & Howlett, M. (2014). Understanding the pre-conditions of commons governance: The role of network management. *Environmental Science & Policy,* 36, 37–47.

Gilligan, C. (1982) *In a Different Voice: Psychological Theory and Women's Development.* Harvard University Press, Cambridge, Mass.

Gilligan, C. (1993). *In a Different Voice: Psychological Theory and Women's Development.* Harvard University Press, Cambridge, Mass.

Gladwin, D. (2020) Digital storytelling going viral: using narrative empathy to promote environmental action. *Media Practice and Education,* 21(4), 275–288. DOI:10.1080/25741136.2020.1832827

González, E. R., Lejano, R. P., Vidales, G., Conner, R. F., Kidokoro, Y., Fazeli, B., & Cabrales, R. (2007). Participatory action research for environmental health: Encountering Freire in the urban barrio. *Journal of Urban Affairs*, 29(1), 77–100.

Goodall, J. (1986). *The Chimpanzees of Gombe: Patterns of Behaviour*. Harvard University Press, Cambridge, Mass.

Gouldner, A. W. (1960). The norm of reciprocity: A preliminary statement. *American Sociological Review*, 25(2), 161–78.

Granovetter, M. (1985). Economic action and social structure: The problem of embeddedness. *American Journal of Sociology*, 91, 481–510.

Graziano, W. G., Habashi, M. M., Sheese, B. E., & Tobin, R. M. (2007). Agreeableness, empathy, and helping: A person× situation perspective. *Journal of Personality and Social Psychology*, 93(4), 583.

Green, M. C., & Brock, T. C. (2000). The role of transportation in the persuasiveness of public narratives. *Journal of Personality and Social Psychology*, 79, 701–721

Grossman, P. J., & Eckel, C. C. (2015). Giving versus taking for a cause. *Economics Letters*, 132(July), 28–30.

Gu, X., Gao, Z., Wang, X., Liu, X., Knight, R. T., Hof, P. R., & Fan, J. (2012). Anterior insular cortex is necessary for empathetic pain perception. *Brain*, 135(9), 2726–2735.

Gubler, M., Brügger, A., & Eyer, M. (2019). Adolescents' perceptions of the psychological distance to climate change, its relevance for building concern about it, and the potential for education. In Filho and Helmstock (Eds.), *Climate Change and the Role of Education* (pp. 129–147). Springer Nature, Cham, Switzerland.

Guilbeault, D., Becker, J., & Centola, D. (2018). Social learning and partisan bias in the interpretation of climate trends. *Proceedings of the National Academy of Sciences*, 115(39), 9714–9719.

Gutiérrez, N. L., Hilborn, R., & Defeo, O. (2011). Leadership, social capital and incentives promote successful fisheries. *Nature*, 470(7334), 386–389.

Gutierrez-Velez, V. H., & MacDicken, K. (2008). Quantifying the direct social and governmental costs of illegal logging in the Bolivian, Brazilian, and Peruvian Amazon. *Forest Policy and Economics*, 10(4), 248–256.

Habermas, J. (1984). *The Theory of Communicative Action* (Vol. 2). Beacon Press, Boston, Mass.

Hafstead, M. (2019). Carbon Pricing 101. Online article (June 6, 2019; updated March 3, 2020) at www.rff.org/publications/explainers/carbon-pricing-101/. Accessed on June 1, 2022.

Hahn, E. R., & Garrett, M. K. (2017). Preschoolers' moral judgments of environmental harm and the influence of perspective taking. *Journal of Environmental Psychology*, 53, 11–19.

Hamilton, J. T. (1995). Pollution as news: Media and stock market reactions to the toxics release inventory data. *Journal of Environmental Economics and Management*, 28(1), 98–113.

Hand, L. C. (2021). A virtuous hearer: An exploration of epistemic injustice and an ethic of care in public encounters. *Administrative Theory & Praxis*, 43(1), 117–133.

Harbaugh, W. T., Mayr, U., & Burghart, D. R. (2007). Neural responses to taxation and voluntary giving reveal motives for charitable donations. *Science*, 316(5831), 1622–1625.

Hardin, G. (1968). The tragedy of the commons. *Science*, 162(3859), 1243–1248.

Harris, A. C., & Madden, G. J. (2002). Delay discounting and performance on the prisoner's dilemma game. *The Psychological Record*, 52, 429–440.

Harrod, H. L. (2000). *The Animals Came Dancing: Native American Sacred Ecology and Animal Kinship*. University of Arizona Press.

Harvey, D. (2009). *Social Justice and the City*. University of Georgia, Athens.

Heinz, N., & Koessler, A. K. (2021). Other-regarding preferences and pro-environmental behaviour: An interdisciplinary review of experimental studies. *Ecological Economics*, 184, 106987.

Henrich, J. P., Boyd, R., Bowles, S., Fehr, E., Camerer, C., & Gintis, H. (Eds.), (2004). *Foundations of Human Sociality: Economic Experiments and Ethnographic Evidence from Fifteen Small-scale Societies*. Oxford University Press, Oxford.

Hernández, B., Suárez, E., Corral-Verdugo, V., & Hess, S. (2012). The relationship between social and environmental interdependence as an explanation of proenvironmental behavior. *Human Ecology Review*, 19(1), 1–9.

Hernández, D., Chang, D., Hutchinson, C., Hill, E., Almonte, A., Burns, R., ... & Evans, D. (2018). Public housing on the periphery: Vulnerable residents and depleted resilience reserves post-hurricane sandy. *Journal of Urban Health*, 95(5), 703–715.

Hess, C., & Ostrom, E. (2005). A Framework for Analyzing the Knowledge Commons: A chapter from Understanding Knowledge as a Commons: From Theory to Practice.

Hibbert, S., Smith, A., Davies, A., & Ireland, F. (2007). Guilt appeals: Persuasion knowledge and charitable giving. *Psychology & Marketing* 24(8), 723–742.

Hirsh, J. B., & Dolderman, D. (2007). Personality predictors of consumerism and environmentalism: A preliminary study. *Personality and individual differences*, 43(6), 1583–1593.

Hoffman, E., McCabe, K., & Smith, V. L. (1996). Social distance and other-regarding behavior in dictator games. *The American Economic Review*, 86(3), 653–660.

Hofmokl, J. (2010). The Internet commons: Towards an eclectic theoretical framework. *International Journal of the Commons*, 4(1), 226–250.

Hollstein, B. (2011). Qualitative Approaches. *The Sage Handbook of Social Network Analysis*, 404–416.

Homer-Dixon, T. F. (2010). Environment, scarcity, and violence. In *Environment, Scarcity, and Violence*. Princeton University Press, Princeton, NJ.

Horkheimer, M., & Adorno, T. W. (1972). *Dialectic of Enlightenment: Max Horkheimer and Theodor W. Adorono*. Seabury Press, New York.

Hourdequin, M. (2010). Climate, collective action and individual ethical obligations. *Environmental Values*, 19(4), 443–464.

Howlett, M. (2019). *Designing Public Policies: Principles and Instruments*. Routledge, New York.

Howlett, M., Mukherjee, I., & Woo, J. J. (2018). Thirty years of research on policy instruments. In *Handbook on Policy, Process and Governing*. Edward Elgar Publishing, Cheltenham, UK.

Hulme, M. (2021). *Climate (Key Ideas in Geography)*. Routledge, New York.

Ingram, M., Ingram, H., & Lejano, R. (2019). Environmental action in the Anthropocene: The power of narrative-networks. *Journal of Environmental Policy & Planning*, 21(5), 492–503.

IPCC (2022). Summary for policymakers. In H.-O. Pörtner, D. C. Roberts, E. S. Poloczanska, K. Mintenbeck, M. Tignor, A. Alegría, M. Craig, S. Langsdorf, S. Löschke, V. Möller, & A. Okem (Eds.), *Climate Change 2022: Impacts, Adaptation, and Vulnerability.* Contribution of Working Group II to the Sixth Assessment Report of the Intergovernmental Panel on Climate Change [H.-O. Pörtner, D. C. Roberts, M. Tignor, E. S. Poloczanska, K. Mintenbeck, A. Alegría, M. Craig, S. Langsdorf, S. Löschke, V. Möller, A. Okem, B. Rama (Eds.), Cambridge University Press, Cambridge and New York.

IPS, Innovate Public Schools (2019). SELA Rising, Fighting for Educational Justice for Latino Students in Southeast Los Angeles, Innovate Public Schools, Los Angeles at https://innovateschools.org/wp-content/uploads/2019/12/SELA-Rising-Final-Report-2019_English_compressed.pdf. Accessed June 1, 2022.

Jager, W., Janssen, M. A., De Vries, H. J. M., De Greef, J., & Vlek, C. A. J. (2000). Behaviour in commons dilemmas: Homo economicus and Homo psychologicus in an ecological-economic model. *Ecological Economics*, 35(3), 357–379.

Jamieson, K. H., & Cappella, J. N. (2008). *Echo Chamber: Rush Limbaugh and the Conservative Media Establishment.* Oxford University Press, Oxford.

Janssen, M. A., & Anderies, J. M. (2011). Governing the commons: Learning from field and laboratory experiments. *Ecological Economics*, 70(9), 1569–1620.

Johnson, S. C., Baxter, L. C., Wilder, L. S., Pipe, J. G., Heiserman, J. E., & Prigatano, G. P. (2002). Neural correlates of self-reflection. *Brain*, 125, 1808–1814.

Johnston, B. M., & Glasford, D. E. (2018). Intergroup contact and helping: How quality contact and empathy shape outgroup helping. *Group Processes & Intergroup Relations*, 21(8), 1185–1201.

Jones, C., Hine, D. W., & Marks, A. D. (2017). The future is now: Reducing psychological distance to increase public engagement with climate change. *Risk Analysis*, 37(2), 331–341. doi.org/10.1111/risa.12601.

Kahneman, D., Ritov, I., Schkade, D., Sherman, S. J., & Varian, H. R. (1999). Economic preferences or attitude expressions?: An analysis of dollar responses to public issues. In *Elicitation of Preferences* (pp. 203–242). Springer, Dordrecht.

Kapembwa, J., & Wells, J. (2016). Climate justice for wildlife: A rights-based account. Intervention or protest: Acting for nonhuman animals, 359–390.

Keller, A., Marsh, J. E., Richardson, B. H., & Ball, L. J. (2022). A systematic review of the psychological distance of climate change: Towards the development of an evidence-based construct. *Journal of Environmental Psychology*, 81, 101822.

Keohane, R. O., & Victor, D. G. (2016). Cooperation and discord in global climate policy. *Nature Climate Change*, 6(6), 570–575.

Keysers, C., & Gazzola, V. (2006). Towards a unifying neural theory of social cognition. *Progress in Brain Research*, 156, 379–401.

Klijn E. H., & Koppenjan J. F. (2000). Public management and policy networks: Foundations of a network approach to governance *Public Management: An International Journal of Research and Theory*, 2(2): 135–158.

Klimecki, O. M., Leiberg, S., Ricard, M., & Singer, T. (2014). Differential pattern of functional brain plasticity after compassion and empathy training. *Social Cognitive and Affective Neuroscience*, 9(6), 873–879.

Kogut, T., & Ritov, I. (2005). The "identified victim" effect: An identified group, or just a single individual? *Journal of Behavioral Decision Making*, 18(3), 157–167.

Kogut, T., & Ritov, I. (2011). Chapter 8. The identifiable victim effect: Causes and boundary conditions. In Oppenheimer, D. M., & C. Y. Olivola (Eds.), *The Science of Giving: Experimental Approaches to the Study of Charity* (pp. 133–148). Psychology Press, New York.

Kohlberg, L. (1974). The claim to moral adequacy of a highest stage of moral judgment. *The Journal of Philosophy*, 70(18), 630–646.

Kohler-Evans, P., & Candice D. B. (2015) "Compassion: How do you teach it?" *Journal of Education and Practice*, 6(11), 33–37. doi: 2222–288X.

Koliba C., & Koppenjan J. (2016). Managing networks and complex adaptive systems. In Bovaird, T., & Loeffler, E. (Eds.), *Public Management and Governance* (pp. 262–274). Routledge, London.

Koliba C. J., Meek J. W., Zia A., & Mills R. W. (2017). *Governance Networks in Public Administration and Public Policy*. Routledge, New York.

Kolleck, N., Well, M., Sperzel, S., & Jörgens, H. (2017). The power of social networks: How the UNFCCC secretariat creates momentum for climate education. *Global Environmental Politics*, 17(4), 106–126.

Krupp, D. B., DeBruine, L. M., & Barclay, P. (2008). A cue of kinship promotes cooperation for the public good. *Evolution and Human Behavior*, 29, 49–55.

Kumar, S. (2004). Victims of gas leak in Bhopal seek redress on compensation. *British Medical Journal*, 2004, 329. doi: https://doi.org/10.1136/bmj.329.7462.366-b (Published 12 August 2004).

Ladak, A., Wilks, M., & Anthis, J. R. (2021). Extending Perspective Taking to Non-Human Groups. Preprint www.sentienceinstitute.org/downloads/Perspective%20taking%20and%20on%20nonhuman%20groups%20-%20preprint.pdf. Accessed June 1, 2022.

Laird-Benner, W., & Ingram, H. (2010). Sonoran desert network weavers: Surprising environmental successes on the US/Mexico Border. *Environment*, 53(1), 6–17.

Lame, D., John, F., & Erdoes, R. (1972). *Lame Deer, Seeker of Visions, Life of a Sioux Medicine Man*, Simon & Schuster, New York.

Lamm, C., Batson, C. D., & Decety, J. (2007). The neural substrate of human empathy: Effects of perspective-taking and cognitive appraisal. *Journal of Cognitive Neuroscience*, 19(1), 42–58.

Lamm, C., Meltzoff, A. N., & Decety, J. (2010). How do we empathize with someone who is not like us? A functional magnetic resonance imaging study. *Journal of Cognitive Neuroscience*, 22(2), 362–376.

Lamm, C., Nusbaum, H. C., Meltzoff, A. N., & Decety, J. (2007). What are you feeling? Using functional magnetic resonance imaging to assess the modulation of sensory and affective responses during empathy for pain. *PLoS One*, 2(12), e1292.

Lee, J. A., & Murnighan, J. K. (2001). The empathy-prospect model and the choice to help. *Journal of Applied Social Psychology*, 31(4), 816–839.

Lee, T., & Van de Meene, S. (2012). Who teaches and who learns? Policy learning through the C40 cities climate network. *Policy Sciences*, 45(3), 199–220.

Leiserowitz, A. (2006). Climate change risk perception and policy preferences: The role of affect, imagery, and values. *Climatic Change*, 77(1), 45–72.

Leiserowitz, A. (2019). 17. Building public and political will for climate change action. In *A Better Planet* (pp. 155–162). Yale University Press, New Haven, Connecticut.

Lejano, R. (2006). *Frameworks for Policy Analysis: Merging Text and Context*. Routledge, New York.

Lejano, R. (2007). *Peace Games: Theorizing about Transboundary Conservation. Peace Parks: Conservation and Conflict Resolution* (pp. 41–54). MIT Press, Cambridge, Mass.

Lejano, R. (2008). The phenomenon of collective action: Modeling institutions as structures of care. *Public Administration Review*, 68(3), 491–504.

Lejano, R. (2023). Economies with other-regarding actors: An exploration (in process).

Lejano, R. P., & Kan, W. S. (2022a). *Relationality: The Inner Life of Public Policy*. Cambridge University Press, Cambridge. Open access book: www.cambridge.org/core/elements/relationality/609FF3DF88BCADAA726208EE3E6F536E

Lejano, R. P., & Kan, W. S. (2022b). IPCC and the City: The need to transition from ideology to climate justice. Journal of Planning Education and Research (online).

Lejano, R. P. (2006). Theorizing peace parks: Two models of collective action. *Journal of Peace Research*, 43(5), 563–581.

Lejano, R. P. (2017). Assemblage and relationality in social-ecological systems. *Dialogues in Human Geography*, 7(2), 192–196.

Lejano, R. P. (2019a). Relationality and social-ecological systems: Going beyond or behind sustainability and resilience. *Sustainability*, 11(10), 2760.

Lejano, R. P. (2019b). Ideology and the narrative of climate skepticism. *Bulletin of the American Meteorological Society*, 100(12), ES415-ES421.

Lejano, R. P. (2021). Relationality: An alternative framework for analysing policy. *Journal of Public Policy*, 41(2), 360–383.

Lejano, R. P., & Ingram, H. (2009). Collaborative networks and new ways of knowing. *Environmental Science & Policy*, 12(6), 653–662.

Lejano, R. P., & Ingram, H. (2012). Modeling the commons as a game with vector payoffs. *Journal of Theoretical Politics*, 24(1), 66–89.

Lejano, R. P., & Nero, S. J. (2020). *The Power of Narrative: Climate Skepticism and the Deconstruction of Science*. Oxford University Press, New York, USA.

Lejano, R. P., Araral, E., & Araral, D. (2014). Interrogating the commons: Introduction to the special issue. Reflecting on a legacy. *Environmental Sciences and Policy*, 36, 1–7.

Lejano, R. P., Ingram, H. M., Whiteley, J. M., Torres, D., & Agduma, S. J. (2007). The importance of context: Integrating resource conservation with local institutions. *Society & Natural Resources*, 20(2), 177–185.

Lejano, R., Chui, E., Lam, T., & Wong, J. (2018). Collective action as narrativity and praxis: Theory and application to Hong Kong's urban protest movements. *Public Policy and Administration*, 33(3), 260–289.

Lejano, R., Guo, J., Lian, H., & Yin, B. (2018). *A Phenomenology of Institutions: Relationality and Governance in China and Beyond*. Routledge, New York.

Lejano, R., Ingram, M., & Ingram, H. (2013). *The Power of Narrative in Environmental Networks*. MIT Press, Cambridge, Mass.

Lejano, R., Ingram, M., & Ingram, H. (2018). Narrative in the policy process. In *Handbook on Policy, Process and Governing* (pp. 309–326). Edward Elgar Publishing, Cheltenham, UK.

Lejano, R., Kan, W., & Chau, C. (2020). "The hidden disequities of carbon trading: Carbon emissions, air toxics, and environmental justice," Frontiers in Environmental Science (online) doi.org/10.3389/fenvs.2020.593014.

Levinas, E. (1961). Totality and infinity: An essay on exteriority (trans: Lingis, Alphonso).

Lévi-Strauss, C. (1966). *The Savage Mind*. University of Chicago Press, Chicago.

Levitt, S. D., & List, J. A. (2007). What do laboratory experiments measuring social preferences reveal about the real world? *Journal of Economic Perspectives*. 21(2):153–174.

Lindeboom, W., Alam, N., Begum, D., & Streatfield, P. K. (2012). The association of meteorological factors and mortality in rural Bangladesh, 1983–2009. *Global Health Action*, 5:61–73.

Loreman, T. (2011). Kindness and empathy in pedagogy. In *Love as Pedagogy* (pp. 15–31). SensePublishers.

Lorenzoni, I., & N. Pidgeon (2006). Public views on climate change: European and USA perspectives. *Climatic Change*, 77:73–95.

Lu, H. (2021). Exposure to victim portrayals: The role of multiple emotions in influencing collective action intentions for environmental justice. *Journal of Environmental Studies and Sciences*, 11(4), 548–560.

Maiella, R., La Malva, P., Marchetti, D., Pomarico, E., Di Crosta, A., Palumbo, R., ... & Verrocchio, M. C. (2020a). The psychological distance and climate change: A systematic review on the mitigation and adaptation behaviors. *Frontiers in Psychology*, 2459.

Maiella, R., La Malva, P., Marchetti, D., Pomarico, E., Di Crosta, A., Palumbo, R., ... & Verrocchio, M. C. (2020b). The psychological distance and climate change: A systematic review on the mitigation and adaptation behaviors. *Frontiers in Psychology*, 11:568899

Majdandžić, J., Amashaufer, S., Hummer, A., Windischberger, C., & Lamm, C. (2016). The selfless mind: How prefrontal involvement in mentalizing with similar and dissimilar others shapes empathy and prosocial behavior. *Cognition*, 157, 24–38.

Mandalaki, E., & Fotaki, M. (2020). The bodies of the commons: Towards a relational embodied ethics of the commons. *Journal of Business Ethics*, 166(4), 745–760.

Mansbridge, J. (2014). The role of the state in governing the commons. *Environmental Science & Policy*, 36, 8–10.

Mansbridge, J. J. (1990). On the relation of altruism and self-interest. In Mansbridge, J. J. (Ed.), *Beyond Self-interest*. University of Chicago Press, Chicago.

Mansbridge, J. J. (Ed.), (1990). *Beyond Self-interest*. University of Chicago Press, Chicago.

Marcuse, H. (1964). *One-Dimensional Man: Studies in the Ideology of Advanced Industrial Society*. Beacon Press, Boston.

Margaret, J., & King, M. J. (1996). The audience in the wilderness: The Disney nature films. *Journal of Popular Film and Television* 24.2, 60–68.

Markowitz, E. M., Slovic, P., Västfjäll, D., & Hodges, S. D. (2013). Compassion fade and the challenge of environmental conservation. *Judgment and Decision making*, 8(4), 397–406.

Mayer, F. S., & C. M. Frantz (2004). The connectedness to nature scale: A measure of individuals' feeling in community with nature. *Journal of Environmental Psychology* 24(4): 503–15.

McClough, D., Ewing, R., & Schertzer, S. (2015). To pay or not to pay: An empirical examination of the effect of injunctive norms on charitable donations. *The Journal of Economics and Politics*, 22(1), 99–118.

McCreary, J. J., Marchant, G. J., & Davis, A. S. (April, 2018). The anatomy of empathy. In Annual Meeting of the American Educational Research Association, New York.

McCright, A. M., & Dunlap, R. E. (2011). The politicization of climate change and polarization in the American public's views of global warming, 2001–2010. *The Sociological Quarterly*, 52(2), 155–194.

McDonald, R. I., Chai, H. Y., & Newell, B. R. (2015). Personal experience and the 'psychological distance' of climate change: An integrative review. *Journal of Environmental Psychology*, 44, 109–118.

McGinnis, M., & Ostrom, E. (1992). Design principles for local and global commons. *The International Political Economy and International Institutions*, 2, 465–493.

McPherson, J. M. (1997). *For Cause and Comrades: Why Men Fought in the Civil War*. Oxford University Press, Oxford.

Meinshausen, M., Lewis, J., McGlade, C., Gütschow, J., Nicholls, Z., Burdon, R., … & Hackmann, B. (2022). Realization of Paris Agreement pledges may limit warming just below 2° C. *Nature*, 604(7905), 304–309.

Miele, M., Wilder, M., Ingram, M., Migrane, E., Schein, R., & Prytherch, D. (2015). The power of narrative in environmental networks (2013), by Lejano, R., Ingram, M., & Ingram, H. [Book Review]. *AAG Annals Review of Books*, 3(2), 99–108.

Mifune, N., Hashimoto, H., & Yamagishi, T. (2010). Altruism toward in-group members as a reputation mechanism. *Evolution and Human Behavior*, 31(2), 109–117.

Militz, T. A., & Foale, S. (2017). The "Nemo Effect": Perception and reality of Finding Nemo's impact on marine aquarium fisheries. *Fish and Fisheries*, 18(3), 596–606.

Mill, J. S. (1859, 2002). On Liberty. published in 2002 by Dover Publications, Mineola, New York. Originally published in 1859 by J. W. Parker, London.

Miller, D. T. (1977). Personal deserving versus justice for others: An exploration of the justice motive. *Journal of Experimental Social Psychology*, 13: 1–13.

Miller, D. T., & Prentice, D. A. (2016). Changing norms to change behavior. *Annual Review of Psychology*, 67, 339–361.

Miller, J. J., Cooley, M., Niu, C., Segress, M., Fletcher, J., Bowman, K., & Littrell, L. (2019). Support, information seeking, and homophily in a virtual support group for adoptive parents: Impact on perceived empathy. *Children and Youth Services Review*, 101, 151–156.

Miralles, A., Raymond, M., & Lecointre, G. (2019). Empathy and compassion toward other species decrease with evolutionary divergence time. *Scientific Reports*, 9(1), 1–8.

Mirra, N. (2018). *Educating for Empathy: Literacy Learning and Civic Engagement*. Teachers College Press, New York.

Morell, M. F. (2014). 8 Governance of Online Creation Communities for the Building of Digital Commons: Viewed through the. Governing knowledge commons, 281.

Morrissey, L., & Boswell, J. (2023). Finding common ground. *European Journal of Political Theory*, 22(1), 141–160.

Mulgan G. (2012). Government with the people: The outlines of a relational state. In Cooke, G., & Muir, R. (Eds.), *The Relational State: How Recognising the Importance of Human Relationship could Revolutionise the Role of the State*. Institute for Public Policy Research, London.

Mumford, L. (1961). *The City in History: Its Origins, Its Transformations, and Its Prospects (Vol. 67)*. Houghton Mifflin Harcourt, New York.

Munson, S., Kotcher, J., Maibach, E., Rosenthal, S. A., & Leiserowitz, A. (2021). The role of felt responsibility in climate change political participation. *Oxford Open Climate Change*, 1(1), kgab012.

Naegele, H. (2020). Where does the Fair Trade money go? How much consumers pay extra for Fair Trade coffee and how this value is split along the value chain. *World Development*, 133, 105006.

Nakagawa, Y., & Saijo, T. (2021). A visual narrative for taking future generations' perspectives. *Sustainability Science*, 16(3), 983–1000.

Nash, J. (1950). Non-Cooperative Games. A Dissertation Presented to the Faculty of Princeton University in Candidacy for the Degree of Doctor of Philosophy. Princeton University, Princeton.

Nash, J. (1951). Non-cooperative games. *Annals of Mathematics*, 286–295.

Natarajan, U. (2021). Environmental justice in the Global South. In Atapattu, S. A., Gonzalez, C. G., & Seck, S. L. (Eds.), *The Cambridge Handbook of Environmental Justice and Sustainable Development*. Cambridge University Press, Cambridge.

Nayak, P. K., & Berkes, F. (2022). Evolutionary Perspectives on the Commons: A Model of Commonisation and Decommonisation. *Sustainability*, 14(7), 4300.

Nieto-Romero, M., Valente, S., Figueiredo, E., & Parra, C. (2019). Historical commons as sites of transformation. A critical research agenda to study human and more-than-human communities. *Geoforum*, 107, 113–123.

Nobis, N. (2009). The "Babe" vegetarians: Bioethics, animal minds and moral methodology. In S. Shapshay (Ed.), *Bioethics at the Movies* (pp. 56–73). Johns Hopkins University Press, Baltimore.

Noddings, N. (1995). Teaching themes of care. *Phi Delta Kappan*, 76, 675–675.

Noddings, N. (2013). *Caring: A Relational Approach to Ethics and Moral Education*. University of California Press, Berkeley.

Nussbaum, M. C. (1990). *Love's Knowledge: Essays on Philosophy and Literature*, Oxford University Press, Oxford and New York.

O'Connell, S. M. (1995). Empathy in chimpanzees: Evidence for theory of mind? *Primates*, 36(3), 397–410.

O'Dell L. 2008. Representations of the "damaged" child: "child saving" in a British children's charity ad campaign. *Children and Society* 22: 383–392. DOI:10.1111/j.1099-0860.2007.00114.x

Ogunseitan, O. A. (2005). Topophilia and the quality of life. *Environmental Health Perspectives*, 113(2), 143–148.

Olson, M. (1965). *The Logic of Collective Action*. Harvard University Press, Cambridge, Mass.

Ortiz-Riomalo, J. F., Koessler, A. K., & Engel, S. (2021). Inducing perspective-taking for prosocial behaviour in natural resource management. Available at SSRN 3773752.

Ostrom, E. (1987). Institutional arrangements for resolving the commons dilemma: Some contending approaches. Conference paper. Conference:The Question of the Commons. The Culture and Ecology of Communal Resources, 46th National Conference of the American Society for Public Administration, Indianapolis, Indiana, March 23–27, 1985, 250–265.

Ostrom, E. (1990). *Governing the Commons: The Evolution of Institutions for Collective Action*. Cambridge University Press, Cambridge and New York.

Ostrom, E. (2000). Crowding out citizenship. *Scandinavian Political Studies*, 23(1), 3–16.

Ostrom, E. (2010). Beyond markets and states: Polycentric governance of complex economic systems. *American Economic Review*, 100(3), 641–672.

Ostrom, E., & Janssen, M. A. (2004). Multi-level governance and resilience of social-ecological systems. In *Globalisation, Poverty and Conflict* (pp. 239–259). Springer, Dordrecht.

Ostrom, E., Gardner, R., Walker, J., Agrawal, A., & Runge, C. F. (1995). Rules, games, and common-pool resources. *Journal of Economic Literature*, 33(3), 1393–1393.

Ostrom, E., Gardner, R., Walker, J., Walker, J. M., & Walker, J. (1994). *Rules, Games, and Common-pool Resources*. University of Michigan Press, Ann Arbor.

Ostrom, E., & Nagendra, H., 2006. Insights on linking forests, trees, and people from the air, on the ground, and in the laboratory. *Proceedings of the National Academy of Sciences* 103(51), 19, 224–19, 331.

Ostrom, V. (1999) "Polycentricity." In M. McGinnis (Ed.), *Polycentricity and Local Public Economies: Readings from the Workshop in Political Theory and Policy Analysis* (pp. 52–74). University of Michigan Press, Ann Arbor.

Pagdee, A., Kim, Y.-S., & Daugherty, P. J., 2006. What makes community forest management successful: A meta-study from community forests throughout the world. *Society and Natural Resources* 19(1), 33–52.

Pahl, S., & Bauer, J. (2013). Overcoming the distance: Perspective taking with future humans improves environmental engagement. *Environment and Behavior*, 45(2), 155–169.

Paul, E. S., & Serpell, J. A. (1996). Obtaining a new pet dog: Effects on middle childhood children and their families. *Applied Animal Behaviour Science*, 47, 17–29.

Perez-Rodriguez, M. M., Mahon, K., Russo, M., Ungar, A. K., & Burdick, K. E. (2015). Oxytocin and social cognition in affective and psychotic disorders. *European Neuropsychopharmacology*, 25(2), 265–282.

Perez-Rodriguez, M. M., Mahon, K., Russo, M., Ungar, A. K., & Burdick, K. E. (2015). Oxytocin and social cognition in affective and psychotic disorders. *European Neuropsychopharmacology*, 25(2), 265–282.

Peth, D., Mußhoff, O., Funke, K., & Hirschauer, N. (2018). Nudging farmers to comply with water protection rules-experimental evidence from Germany. *Ecological Economics*, 152, 310–321.

Pfattheicher, S., Sassenrath, C., & S. Schindler (2016). Feelings for the suffering of others and the environment: Compassion fosters proenvironmental tendencies. *Environment and Behavior*, 48(7).

Pilny, A., Poole, M. S., Reichelmann, A., & Klein, B. (2017). A structurational group decision-making perspective on the commons dilemma: Results from an online public goods game. *Journal of Applied Communication Research*, 45(4), 413–428.

Polletta, F. (1998). Contending stories: Narrative in social movements. *Qualitative Sociology* 21(4), 419–446.

Polski, M. M., & Ostrom, E. (2017). An institutional framework for policy analysis and design. In Cole, D. H., & McGinnis, M. D. (Eds.), *Elinor Ostrom and the Bloomington School of Political Economy: A Framework for Policy Analysis (Vol. 3)*. Lexington Books, Washington, D.C.

Poteete, A. R., Janssen, M. A., & Ostrom, E. (2010). *Working Together: Collective Action, the Commons, and Multiple Methods in Practice*. Princeton University Press, Princeton, NJ.

Powell Walter, W. (1990). Neither market nor hierarchy: Network forms of organization. *Research in Organizational Behavior*, 12(2), 295–336.

Preis, M. A., Kröner-Herwig, B., Schmidt-Samoa, C., Dechent, P., & Barke, A. (2015). Neural correlates of empathy with pain show habituation eects. An fMRI study. *PLoS One*, 10, e0137056. doi: 10.1371/journal.pone.0137056

Preston, S. D., & de Waal, F. B. M. (2002). Empathy: Its ultimate and proximate bases. *Behavioural and Brain Sciences*, 25, 1–72.

Preston, S. D., Liao, J. D., Toombs, T. P., Romero-Canyas, R., Speiser, J., & Seifert, C. M. (2021). A case study of a conservation flagship species: The monarch butterfly. *Biodiversity and Conservation*, 30(7), 2057–2077.

Prguda, E., & Neumann, D. L. (2014). Inter-human and animal-directed empathy: A test for evolutionary biases in empathetic responding. *Behavioural processes*, 108, 80–86.

Prokop, P., & Tunnicliffe, S. D. (2010). Effects of having pets at home on children's attitudes toward popular and unpopular animals. *Anthrozoös*, 23(1), 21–35.

Prokop, P., Prokop, M., & Tunnicliffe, S. D. (2008). Effects of keeping animals as pets on children's concepts of vertebrates and invertebrates. *International Journal of Science Education*, 30, 431–449.

Proshansky, H. M., Fabian, A. K., & Kaminoff, R. (1983). Place-identity: Physical world socialization of the self. *Journal of Environmental Psychology*, 3(1), 57–83.

Provan, K. G., & Kenis, P. (2008). Modes of network governance: Structure, management, and effectiveness. *Journal of Public Administration Research and Theory*, 18(2), 229–252.

Pulido, L. (2015). Geographies of race and ethnicity: White supremacy vs white privilege in environmental racism research. *Progress in Human Geography*, 39(6), 809–17.

Rabe, B. G. (2018). *Can We Price Carbon?* MIT Press, Cambridge.

Rabin, M. (1993). Incorporating fairness into game theory and economics. *The American Economic Review*, 83(5), 1281–1302.

Rabinovich, A., Morton, T. A., Postmes, T., & Verplanken, B. (2009). Think global, act local: The effect of goal and mindset specificity on willingness to donate to an environmental organization. *Journal of Environmental Psychology*, 29, 391e399.

Rapley, J. (2013). *Understanding Development: Theory and Practice in the Third World*. Routledge, New York.

Rapoport, A. (1974). Prisoner's dilemma – recollections and observations. In *Game Theory as a Theory of a Conflict Resolution* (pp. 17–34). Springer, Dordrecht.

Rawls, J. (1971). *A Theory of Justice*. Belknap Press, Cambridge, Mass.

Reddy, S. (2018). "Plastic Pollution Affects Sea Life Throughout the Ocean," Pew Charitable Trusts online report, at www.pewtrusts.org/en/research-and-analysis/articles/2018/09/24/plastic-pollution-affects-sea-life-throughout-the-ocean. Accessed September 17, 2021.

Reed, K. A., Wehner, M. F., & Zarzycki, C. M. (2022). Attribution of 2020 hurricane season extreme rainfall to human-induced climate change. *Nature Communications*, 13(1), 1–6.

Rees, W., & Wackernagel, M. (2008). Urban ecological footprints: Why cities cannot be sustainable – and why they are a key to sustainability. In *Urban Ecology* (pp. 537–555). Springer, Boston, MA.

Ricoeur, P. (1976). *Interpretation Theory: Discourse and the Surplus of Meaning*. TCU Press, Fort Worth.

Ricœur, P. (1983). *Time and Narrative (Vols. 1, 2, and 3)*. (trans. K. Blamey and D. Pellauer), University of Chicago Press, Chicago.

Ricoeur, P. (1988). *Time and Narrative (Vol. 3)*. University of Chicago Press, Chicago.

Ricoeur, P. (1991). Narrative identity. *Philosophy Today*, 35(1), 73–81.

Ridley, M. (2003). *The Agile Gene*. HarperCollins, Toronto.

Rilling, J. K., DeMarco, A. C., Hackett, P. D., Thompson, R., Ditzen, B., Patel, R. et al. (2012). Effects of intranasal oxytocin and vasopressin on cooperative behavior and associated brain activity in men. *Psychoneuroendocrinology*, 37, 447–467. doi: 10.1016/j.psyneuen.2011.07.013

Rock, J., & Gilchrist, E. (2021). Creating empathy for the more-than-human under 2 degrees heating. *Journal of Environmental Studies and Sciences*, 1–9.

Rode, J., G'omez-Baggethun, E., Krause, T. (2015). Motivation crowding by economic incentives in conservation policy: A review of the empirical evidence. *Ecological Economics*, 117, 270–282. https://doi.org/10.1016/j.ecolecon.2014.11.019.

Rogers, E. M. (2003). *Diffusion of Innovations*. Free Press, New York.

Rogge, N., Theesfeld, I., & Strassner, C. (2018). Social sustainability through social interaction – a national survey on community gardens in Germany. *Sustainability*, 10(4), 1085.

Rosenbloom, D., Markard, J., Geels, F. W., & Fuenfschilling, L. (2020). Why carbon pricing is not sufficient to mitigate climate change – and how "sustainability transition policy" can help. *Proceedings of the National Academy of Sciences*, 117(16), 8664–8668.

Rubinstein, A. (1979). Equilibrium in supergames with the overtaking criterion. *Journal of Economic Theory*, 21(1), 1–9.

Rumble, A. C., Van Lange, P. A., & Parks, C. D. (2010). The benefits of empathy: When empathy may sustain cooperation in social dilemmas. *European Journal of Social Psychology*, 40(5), 856–866.

Sacchi, S., Riva, P., & Aceto, A. (2016). Myopic about climate change: Cognitive style, psychological distance, and environmentalism. *Journal of Experimental Social Psychology*, 65, 68–73. doi: 10.1016/j.jesp.2016.03.006

Sandström, A., & Rova, C. (2009). The network structure of adaptive governance-A single case study of a fish management area. *International Journal of the Commons*, 4(1).

Sandström, A., 2008. Policy Networks: The Relation Between Structure and Performance. Department of Business Administration and Social Sciences, Lulea? University of Technology, Lulea?, Sweden. Schneider, M., Scholz, J., Lubell, M., Mindruta,

Sandström, E., Ekman, A. K., & Lindholm, K. J. (2017). Commoning in the periphery–The role of the commons for understanding rural continuities and change. *International Journal of the Commons*, 11(1):508–531.

Sarangi, S. (2002). Crimes of Bhopal and the global campaign for justice. *Social Justice*, 29(89), 47–52.

Sassenrath, C., Diefenbacher, S., Pfattheicher, S., & Keller, J. (2021). The potential and limitations of empathy in changing health-relevant affect, cognition and behaviour. *European Review of Social Psychology*, 1–34.

Scannell, L., & Gifford, R. (2011). Personally relevant climate change: The role of place attachment and local versus global message framing in engagement. *Environment and Behavior*, 45(1), 60–85. https://doi.org/10.1177/0013916511421196.

Schelling, T. C. (1968). The life you save may be your own. In Chase, S. (Ed.), *Problems in Public Expenditure Analysis* (pp. 127–162). Brookings Institute, Washington, D.C.

Schilke, O., Reimann, M., & Cook, K. S. (2021). Trust in social relations. *Annual Review of Sociology*, 47, 239–259.

Schlager E. (1999). A comparison of frameworks, theories, and models of policy processes. *Theories of the Policy Process*, 1, 233–260.

Schlager, E., & Cox, M. (2018). The IAD framework and the SES framework: An introduction and assessment of the Ostrom workshop frameworks. In *Theories of the Policy Process* (pp. 215–252). Routledge.

Schlegel, S. A. (2003). *Wisdom from a Rainforest: The Spiritual Journey of an Anthropologist.* University of Georgia Press, Athens, Georgia.

Schmidt, J. J., & Dowsley, M. (2010). Hunting with polar bears: Problems with the passive properties of the commons. *Human Ecology*, 38(3), 377–387.

Schneider, M., Scholz, J., Lubell, M., Mindruta, D., & Edwardsen, M. (2003). Building consensual institutions: Networks and the national estuary program. *American Journal of Political Science*, 47(1), 143–158.

Schön, D. A., & Rein, M. (1994). *Frame Reflection: Toward the Resolution of Intractable Policy Controversies.* Basic Books, New York.

Schuldt, J. P., Rickard, L. N., & Yang, Z. J. (2018). Does reduced psychological distance increase climate engagement? On the limits of localizing climate change. *Journal of Environmental Psychology*, 55, 147–153.

Schultz, P. W. (2000). Empathizing with nature: The effects of perspective taking on concern for environmental issues. *Journal of Social Issues*, 56, 391–406.

Schumann, K., Zaki, J., & Dweck, C. S. (2014). Addressing the empathy deficit: Beliefs about the malleability of empathy predict effortful responses when empathy is challenging. *Journal of Personality and Social Psychology*, 107(3), 475.

Schwan, S., Grajal, A., & Lewalter, D. (2014). Understanding and engagement in places of science experience: Science museums, science centers, zoos, and aquariums. *Educational Psychologist*, 49(2), 70–85.

Schwartz, S. H. (1970). Normative explanations of helping behavior: a critique, proposal, and empirical test. In Macaulay, J., & Berkowitz, L. (Eds.), *Altruism and Helping Behavior.* Academic Press, New York.

Scott, K. E., & Graham, J. A. (2015). Service-learning: Implications for empathy and community engagement in elementary school children. *Journal of Experiential Education*, 38(4), 354–372.

Sen, A. K. (1977). Rational fools: A critique of the behavioral foundations of economic theory. *Philosophy & Public Affairs*, 317–344.

Sen, A. K. (2009). *The Idea of Justice.* Harvard University Press, Cambridge, Mass.

Severson, A. W., & Coleman, E. A. (2015). Moral frames and climate change policy attitudes. *Social Science Quarterly*, 96(5), 1277–1290.

Sevillano, V., Aragonés, J. I., & Schultz, P. W. (2007). Perspective taking, environmental concern, and the moderating role of dispositional empathy. *Environment and Behavior*, 39(5), 685–705.

Shamay-Tsoory, S. G., Aharon-Peretz, J., & Perry, D. (2009). Two systems for empathy: A double dissociation between emotional and cognitive empathy in inferior frontal gyrus versus ventromedial prefrontal lesions. *Brain*, 132(3), 617–627.

Shapiro, I., Richardson, S., McClurg, S., & Sokhey, A. (2020). Discussion networks in political decision making. In Oxford Research Encyclopedia of Politics.

Sheeder, R. J., & Lynne, G. D. (2011). Empathy-conditioned conservation: "Walking in the shoes of others" as a conservation farmer. *Land Economics*, 87(3), 433–452.

Singer T., Seymour B., O'Doherty J. P., Stephan K. E., Dolan R. D. et al. (2006). Empathic neural responses are modulated by the perceived fairness of others. *Nature*, 439, 466–469.

Singh, S. P., & Swanson, M. (2017). How issue frames shape beliefs about the importance of climate change policy across ideological and partisan groups. *PLoS One*, 12(7), e0181401.

Small D, Verrochi N. 2009. The face of need: Facial emotion expression on charity advertisements. *Journal of Marketing Research XLVI* (December), 777–787.

Small, D. A., & Loewenstein, G. (2003). Helping a victim or helping the victim: Altruism and identifiability. *Journal of Risk and Uncertainty*, 26(1), 5–16.

Smith R. J., Verissimo D., Isaac N. J. B., Jones K. E. (2012). Identifying Cinderella species: Uncovering mammals with conservation fagship appeal. *Conservation Letters*, 5, 205–212.

Smith, A. (2006). Cognitive empathy and emotional empathy in human behavior and evolution. *The Psychological Record*, 56(1), 3–21.

Sober, E., & Wilson, D. S. (1999). *Unto Others: The Evolution and Psychology of Unselfish Behavior (No. 218)*. Harvard University Press, Cambridge, Mass.

Sojka, J. R. Z. (1986). *Understanding Donor Behavior: A Classification Paradigm*. ACR North American Advances.

Sontag, S. (2004). *Regarding the Pain of Others*. Penguin, London.

Spence, A., & Pidgeon, N. (2010). Framing and communicating climate change: The effects of distance and outcome frame manipulations. *Global Environmental Change*, 20(4), 656–667.

Spence, A., Poortinga, W., & Pidgeon, N. (2012). The psychological distance of climate change: Psychological distance of climate change. *Risk Analysis*, 32, 957–972. doi: 10.1111/j.1539-6924.2011.01695.x

Spies, M., & Alff, H. (2020). Assemblages and complex adaptive systems: A conceptual crossroads for integrative research? *Geography Compass*, 14(10), e12534.

Spivak, G. C. (2003). Can the subaltern speak? *Die Philosophin*, 14(27), 42–58.

Stanley, S., Millin, P., Mickleson, K., & Milfont, T. L. (2018). Not here, not to us, maybe not at all: The psychological distance of climate change in relation to environmental engagement [Preprint]. PsyArXiv.

Stein, E. (1964). *On the Problem of Empathy*. W. Stein (trans.), Springer-Science+Business Media, The Hague, Netherlands.

Stern, N., S. Peters, V. Bakhshi, A. Bowen, C. Cameron, S. Catovsky et al. (2006). *Stern Review: The Economics of Climate Change*, HM Treasury, London.

Stewart-Williams, S. (2007). Altruism among kin vs. nonkin: Effects of cost of help and reciprocal exchange. *Evolution and Human Behavior*, 28(3), 193–198.

Stocks, E. L., Lishner, D. A., & Decker, S. K. (2009). Altruism or psychological escape: Why does empathy promote prosocial behavior? *European Journal of Social Psychology*, 39(5), 649–665.

Stokols, D. (2018). *Social Ecology in the Digital Age: Solving Complex Problems in a Globalized World*. Academic Press, Cambridge, Mass.

Stokols, D. (2020). Toward an environmental psychology of planetary recovery and biospheric survival. *Umweltpsychologie-German Journal of Environmental Psychology*, 24(2), 12–33.

Stone, D. (2000). Caring by the book. In M. Harrington-Meyer (Ed.), *Care Work: Gender, Labor, and Welfare States* (pp. 89–111). Routledge, New York.

Stout, M., & Love, J. M. (2021). Competing ontologies: A redux primer for public administration. *The American Review of Public Administration*, 51(6), 422–435.

Susskind L. (2006). Arguing, bargaining, and getting agreement. The Oxford handbook of public policy, 269–295.

Susskind, L. E., & Cruikshank, J. L. (2006). *Breaking Roberts Rules: The New Way to Run Your Meeting, Build Consensus, and Get Results.* Oxford University Press., New York.

Susskind, L., & Kim, A. (2022). Building local capacity to adapt to climate change. *Climate Policy*, 22(5), 593–606.

Swim, J. K., & Bloodhart, B. (2015). Portraying the perils to polar bears: The role of empathic and objective perspective-taking toward animals in climate change communication. *Environmental Communication*, 9(4), 446–468.

Sze, J. (2020). *Environmental Justice in a Moment of Danger (Vol. 11).* University of California Press, Berkeley, CA.

Taylor, S. M. (2007) Buffalo hunt: international trade and the virtual extinction of the North American bison. National Bureau of Economic Research Working Paper Series. www.nber.org/papers/w12969 Accessed 28 August 2010.

Tajfel, H., M. G. Billig, R. P. Bundy, & C. Flament (1971). Social categorization and intergroup behaviour. *European Journal of Social Psychology*, 1, 149–178.

Teodoro, J. D., Prell, C., & Sun, L. (2021). Quantifying stakeholder learning in climate change adaptation across multiple relational and participatory networks. *Journal of Environmental Management*, 278, 111508.

Thatchenkery, T. J. (1992). "Organizations as 'Texts': Hermeneutics as a model for understanding organizational change." *Research in Organizational Change and Development* 6:197–233.

Thornton, B., Kirchner, G., & Jacobs, J. (1991). Influence of a photograph on a charitable appeal: A picture may be worth a thousand words when it has to speak for itself. *Journal of Applied Social Psychology*, 21(6), 433–445.

Thushari, G. G. N., & Senevirathna, J. D. M. (2020). Plastic pollution in the marine environment. *Heliyon*, 6(8), e04709.

Tindall, D. B., & Piggot, G. (2015). Influence of social ties to environmentalists on public climate change perceptions. *Nature Climate Change*, 5(6), 546–549.

Tronto, J. (2017). There is an alternative: *Homines curans* and the limits of neo-liberalism. *International Journal of Care and Caring*, 1(1), 27–43.

Trope, Y., & Liberman, N. (2010). Construal-level theory of psychological distance. *Psychological Review* 117, 440–463. doi: 10.1037/a0018963

Tuan, Y. F. (1990). *Topophilia: A Study of Environmental Perception, Attitudes, and Values.* Columbia University Press.

Twenge, J. M., Baumeister, R. F., DeWall, C. N., Ciarocco, N. J., & Bartels, J. M. (2007). Social exclusion decreases prosocial behavior. *Journal of Personality and Social Psychology*, 92(1), 56–66.

UNEP, United Nations Environmental Program (2021). *Emissions Gap Report 2021: The Heat is On – A World of Climate Promises Not Yet Delivered.* United Nations, New York.

Upright, R. L. (2002). To tell a tale: The use of moral dilemmas to increase empathy in the elementary school child. *Early Childhood Education Journal*, 30(1), 15–20.

Vale, M. T., Stanley, J. T., Houston, M. L., Villalba, A. A., & Turner, J. R. (2020). Ageism and behavior change during a health pandemic: A preregistered study. *Frontiers in Psychology*, 11, 3156.

van Klingeren, F., & de Graaf, N. D. (2021). Heterogeneity, trust and common-pool resource management. *Journal of Environmental Studies and Sciences*, 11(1), 37–64.

Van Lange, P. A., & Huckelba, A. L. (2021). Psychological distance: How to make climate change less abstract and closer to the self. *Current Opinion in Psychology*, 42, 49–53.

Van Lange, P. A., De Cremer, D., Van Dijk, E., & Van Vugt, M. (2007). Self-interest and beyond: Basic principles of social interaction.

Villamayor-Tomas, S., Thiel, A., Amblard, L., Zikos, D., & Blanco, E. (2019). Diagnosing the role of the state for local collective action: Types of action situations and policy instruments. *Environmental Science & Policy*, 97, 44–57.

Vygotsky, L. (1987). Zone of proximal development. *Mind in society: The development of higher psychological processes*, 5291, 157.

Vygotsky, L. S. (1978). *Mind in Society* In M. Cole, V. John-Steiner, S. Scribner, & E. Souberman (Eds.), Harvard University Press, Cambridge, Mass.

Walch, C. (2018). Typhoon Haiyan: Pushing the limits of resilience? The effect of land inequality on resilience and disaster risk reduction policies in the Philippines. *Critical Asian Studies*, 50(1), 122–135.

Walker, G. B., Daniels, S. E., & Emborg, J. (2022). Insights and opportunities in public participation practice: Applying collaborative learning in environmental policy decision situations. In Hansen, A., & R. Cox (Eds.), *The Routledge Handbook of Environment and Communication* (pp. 157–180). Routledge, New York.

Walsh, Z., Böhme, J., & Wamsler, C. (2021). Towards a relational paradigm in sustainability research, practice, and education. *Ambio*, 50(1), 74–84.

Wang S., Hurlstone M. J., Leviston Z., Walker I., & Lawrence C. (2019). Climate change from a distance: An analysis of construal level and psychological distance from climate change. *Frontiers in Psychology*, 10, 230. doi: 10.3389/fpsyg.2019.00230

Warner, K. (2020). Climate Justice: Who bears the burden and pays the price? *Social Alternatives*, 39(2), 19–25.

Weber, M. (1920). *The Protestant Ethic and the Spirit of Capitalism*. Scribner's, New York, 1920.

Wei, L., & Liu, B. (2020). Reactions to others' misfortune on social media: Effects of homophily and publicness on schadenfreude, empathy, and perceived deservingness. *Computers in Human Behavior*, 102, 1–13.

West, S., Haider, L. J., Stålhammar, S., & Woroniecki, S. (2020). A relational turn for sustainability science? Relational thinking, leverage points and transformations. *Ecosystems and People*, 16(1), 304–325.

Whatmore, S. (1997). Dissecting the autonomous self: Hybrid cartographies for a relational ethics. *Environment and Planning D: Society and Space*, 15(1), 37–53.

Whitley, C. T., Kalof, L., & Flach, T. (2020). Using animal portraiture to activate emotional affect. Environment and Behavior, 0013916520928429.

Whitley, D. (2008). *The Idea of Nature in Disney Animation*. Ashgate Publishing Limited, England.

Wilhelm, M. O., & Bekkers, R. (2010). Helping behavior, dispositional empathic concern, and the principle of care. *Social Psychology Quarterly*, 73(1), 11–32.

Williamson, O. E. (1985). *The Economic Institutions of Capitalism*. The Free Press, New York.

Wilson, D. S., Van Vugt, M., & O'Gorman, R. (2008). Multilevel selection theory and major evolutionary transitions. *Current Directions in Psychological Science*, 17(1), 6–9.

Winerman, L. (2019). Mourning the land. *Monitor on Psychology*, 50(5), 24. www.apa.org/monitor/2019/05/mourning-land

Wirth, L. (1938). Urbanism as a way of life. *American Journal of Sociology*, 44(1), 1–24.

Witt, J. (2016). Engaging the empathic imagination to explore environmental justice. In *Learner-centered Teaching Activities for Environmental and Sustainability Studies* (pp. 221–226). Springer, Cham.

Wong-Parodi, G., & Feygina, I. (2020). Understanding and countering the motivated roots of climate change denial. *Current Opinion in Environmental Sustainability*, 42, 60–64.

Woodland Park Zoo (2019). March, 2019. www.zoo.org/document.doc?id=2560

Xin, K. K., & Pearce, J. L. (1996). Guanxi: Connections as substitutes for formal institutional support. *Academy of Management Journal*, 39(6): 1641–1658.

Young, A., Khalil, K. A., & Wharton, J. (2018). Empathy for animals: A review of the existing literature. *Curator: The Museum Journal*, 61(2), 327–343.

Yu, R. (2014). Evaluation study on animals Asia's Dr Dog programme animal assisted therapy for senior citizens with dementia, cared for in non government subvented institutions in Hong Kong.

Zagefka, H., & James, T. (2015). The psychology of charitable donations to disaster victims and beyond. *Social Issues and Policy Review*, 9(1), 155–192.

Zak, P. J., Stanton, A. A., & Ahmadi, S. (2007). Oxytocin increases generosity in humans. *PLoS One*, 2(11), e1128.

Zarzycka, M. (2016). Save the child: Photographed faces and affective transactions in NGO child sponsoring programs. *European Journal of Women's Studies*, 23(1), 28–42.

Index